Con
SOUTH CAROLINA
BIRDS

Contributors:

Curtis Smalling, Krista Kagume
& Gregory Kennedy

LONE
PINE

Lone Pine Publishing International

© 2007 Lone Pine Publishing International Inc.
First printed in 2007   10 9 8 7 6 5 4 3 2 1
Printed in China

Distributed by Lone Pine Publishing
1808 B Street NW, Suite 140
Auburn, WA USA 98001

Website: www.lonepinepublishing.com

Library and Archives Canada Cataloguing in Publication

Smalling, Curtis G., 1963–
   Compact guide to South Carolina birds / Curtis G. Smalling,
   Gregory Kennedy.

   Includes bibliographical references and index.
   ISBN-13: 978-976-8200-26-6

   1. Birds—South Carolina—Identification. 2. Bird watching—
South Carolina. I. Kennedy, Gregory, 1956– II. Title.

QL684.S6.S53 2007   598.09757   C2006-903452-4

Illustrations: Gary Ross, Ted Nordhagen, Ewa Pluciennik
Digital Scanning: Elite Lithographers Co.
Egg Photography: Alan Bibby, Gary Whyte

We wish to thank the Royal Alberta Museum for providing access
to their egg collection.

PC: P13

Contents

4 Reference Guide

WATERFOWL

Canada Goose
size 42 in • p. 20

Wood Duck
size 17 in • p. 22

Mallard
size 24 in • p. 24

Northern Pintail
size 23 in • p. 26

Bufflehead
size 14 in • p. 28

Red-breasted Merganser
size 23 in • p. 30

TURKEYS & QUAIL

Wild Turkey
size 36 in • p. 32

Northern Bobwhite
size 10 in • p. 34

Pied-billed Grebe
size 13 in • p. 36

DIVING BIRDS

Northern Gannet
size 36 in • p. 38

Brown Pelican
size 48 in • p. 40

Double-crested Cormorant
size 29 in • p. 42

HERONLIKE BIRDS

Anhinga
size 33 in • p. 44

Great Blue Heron
size 51 in • p. 46

Great Egret
size 39 in • p. 48

Snowy Egret
size 24 in • p. 50

Green Heron
size 18 in • p. 52

Black-crowned Night-Heron
size 24 in • p. 54

HERONLIKE BIRDS

White Ibis
size 22 in • p. 56

Wood Stork
size 38 in • p. 58

Turkey Vulture
size 28 in • p. 60

BIRDS OF PREY

Osprey
size 23 in • p. 62

Mississippi Kite
size 14 in • p. 64

Bald Eagle
size 37 in • p. 66

Red-shouldered Hawk
size 19 in • p. 68

Red-tailed Hawk
size 20 in • p. 70

American Kestrel
size 8 in • p. 72

RAILS & COOTS

Purple Gallinule
size 13 in • p. 74

American Coot
size 14 in • p. 76

Black-bellied Plover
size 12 in • p. 78

SHOREBIRDS

Killdeer
size 10 in • p. 80

American Oystercatcher
size 18 in • p. 82

Greater Yellowlegs
size 14 in • p. 84

Willet
size 15 in • p. 86

Spotted Sandpiper
size 7 in • p. 88

Ruddy Turnstone
size 9 in • p. 90

6 Reference Guide

SHOREBIRDS

Sanderling
size 8 in • p. 92

American Woodcock
size 11 in • p. 94

Laughing Gull
size 16 in • p. 96

GULLS & ALLIES

Ring-billed Gull
size 19 in • p. 98

Royal Tern
size 20 in • p. 100

Black Skimmer
size 18 in • p. 102

DOVES & CUCKOOS

Rock Pigeon
size 12 in • p. 104

Mourning Dove
size 12 in • p. 106

Yellow-billed Cuckoo
size 12 in • p. 108

OWLS

Eastern Screech-Owl
size 8 in • p. 110

Great Horned Owl
size 21 in • p. 112

Chuck-will's-widow
size 12 in • p. 114

NIGHTJARS, SWIFTS & HUMMINGBIRDS

Chimney Swift
size 5 in • p. 116

Ruby-throated Hummingbird
size 4 in • p. 118

Belted Kingfisher
size 13 in • p. 120

WOODPECKERS

Red-headed Woodpecker
size 9 in • p. 122

Downy Woodpecker
size 6 in • p. 124

Northern Flicker
size 13 in • p. 126

Pileated Woodpecker
size 17 in • p. 128

Eastern Wood-Pewee
size 6 in • p. 130

Acadian Flycatcher
size 6 in • p. 132

Great Crested Flycatcher
size 8 in • p. 134

Eastern Kingbird
size 9 in • p. 136

Loggerhead Shrike
size 9 in • p. 138

White-eyed Vireo
size 5 in • p. 140

Red-eyed Vireo
size 6 in • p. 142

Blue Jay
size 12 in • p. 144

American Crow
size 18 in • p. 146

Purple Martin
size 7 in • p. 148

Barn Swallow
size 7 in • p. 150

Carolina Chickadee
size 5 in • p. 152

Tufted Titmouse
size 6 in • p. 154

White-breasted Nuthatch
size 6 in • p. 156

Brown-headed Nuthatch
size 5 in • p. 158

Carolina Wren
size 5 in • p. 160

Marsh Wren
size 5 in • p. 162

KINGLETS, GNATCATCHERS & THRUSHES

Ruby-crowned Kinglet
size 4 in • p. 164

Blue-gray Gnatcatcher
size 5 in • p. 166

Eastern Bluebird
size 7 in • p. 168

Wood Thrush
size 8 in • p. 170

American Robin
size 10 in • p. 172

Gray Catbird
size 9 in • p. 174

MIMICS & STARLINGS

Northern Mockingbird
size 10 in • p. 176

Brown Thrasher
size 11 in • p. 178

European Starling
size 8 in • p. 180

Cedar Waxwing
size 7 in • p. 182

Northern Parula
size 4 in • p. 184

Yellow-rumped Warbler
size 5 in • p. 186

WOOD-WARBLERS & TANAGERS

Yellow-throated Warbler
size 5 in • p. 188

Pine Warbler
size 5 in • p. 190

Common Yellowthroat
size 5 in • p. 192

Hooded Warbler
size 5 in • p. 194

Summer Tanager
size 7 in • p. 196

Eastern Towhee
size 8 in • p. 198

Field Sparrow
size 6 in • p. 200

Seaside Sparrow
size 6 in • p. 202

White-throated Sparrow
size 7 in • p. 204

Dark-eyed Junco
size 6 in • p. 206

Northern Cardinal
size 8 in • p. 208

Indigo Bunting
size 5 in • p. 210

Painted Bunting
size 5 in • p. 212

Red-winged Blackbird
size 8 in • p. 214

Eastern Meadowlark
size 9 in • p. 216

Boat-tailed Grackle
size 15 in • p. 218

Brown-headed Cowbird
size 7 in • p. 220

Orchard Oriole
size 7 in • p. 222

House Finch
size 6 in • p. 224

American Goldfinch
size 5 in • p. 226

House Sparrow
size 6 in • p. 228

SPARROWS, CARDINALS & BUNTINGS

BLACKBIRDS & ALLIES

FINCHLIKE BIRDS

Introduction

If you have ever admired a songbird's pleasant notes, been fascinated by a soaring hawk or wondered how woodpeckers keep sawdust out of their nostrils, this book is for you. There is so much to discover about birds and their surroundings that birding is becoming one of the fastest growing hobbies on the planet. Many people find it relaxing, while others enjoy its outdoor appeal. Some people see it as a way to reconnect with nature, an opportunity to socialize with like-minded people or a way to monitor the environment.

Whether you are just beginning to take an interest in birds or can already identify many species, there is always more to learn. We've highlighted both the remarkable traits and the more typical behaviors displayed by some of our most abundant or noteworthy birds. A few live in specialized habitats, but most are common species that you have a good chance of encountering on most outings or in your backyard.

BIRDING IN SOUTH CAROLINA

We are truly blessed by the geographical and biological diversity of South Carolina. In addition to supporting a wide range of breeding birds and year-round residents, our state hosts a large number of spring and fall migrants

Northern Cardinal

that move through our area on the way to their breeding and wintering grounds. In all, over 420 bird species have been seen and recorded in South Carolina.

Identifying birds in action and under varying conditions involves skill, timing and luck. The more you know about a bird, its range, preferred habitat, food preferences and hours and seasons of activity, the better your chances will be of seeing it. Generally, spring and fall are the busiest birding times. Temperatures are moderate then, many species of birds are on the move, and in spring male songbirds are belting out their unique courtship songs. Birds are usually most active in the early morning hours, except in winter when they forage during the day when milder temperatures prevail.

Another useful clue for correctly recognizing birds is knowledge of their habitat. Simply put, a bird's habitat is the place where it normally lives. Some birds prefer open water, some are found in cattail marshes, others like mature coniferous forest, and still other birds prefer abandoned agricultural fields overgrown with tall grass and shrubs. Habitats are just like neighborhoods: if you associate friends with the suburb in which they live, you can easily learn to associate specific birds with their preferred habitat. Only in migration, especially during inclement weather, do some birds leave their usual habitat.

Recognizing birds by their songs and calls can greatly enhance your birding experience. Numerous tapes and CDs are available to help you learn bird songs, and a portable player with headphones can let you quickly compare a live bird with a recording. The old-fashioned way to remember bird songs is to make up words for them. We have given you some of the classic renderings in the species accounts that follow. Some of these approximations work better than others; birds often add or delete syllables from their calls, and very few pronounce consonants in a recognizable fashion. Remember, too, that songs may vary from place to place.

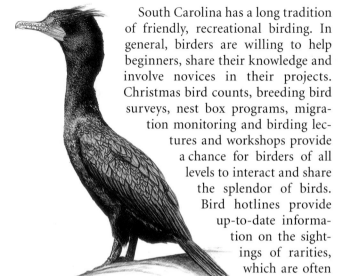

South Carolina has a long tradition of friendly, recreational birding. In general, birders are willing to help beginners, share their knowledge and involve novices in their projects. Christmas bird counts, breeding bird surveys, nest box programs, migration monitoring and birding lectures and workshops provide a chance for birders of all levels to interact and share the splendor of birds. Bird hotlines provide up-to-date information on the sightings of rarities, which are often easier to relocate than you might think.

Double-crested Cormorant

For more information or to participate in these projects, contact the following organizations:

Audubon South Carolina
Website: www.audubon.org/local/sanctuary/beidler/
Phone: 843-462-2160

Cape Romain Bird Observatory
P.O. Box 362
McClellanville, SC 29458
Website: www.crbo.net
Phone: 843-607-0105

The Carolina Bird Club
Website: www.carolinabirdclub.org
Quarterly publication: *The Chat*

Carolinas Rare Bird Alert
Phone: 704-332-2473

BIRD LISTING

Many birders list the species they have seen during excursions or at home. It is up to you to decide what kind of list—systematic or casual—you will keep, and you may choose not to make lists at all. Lists may prove rewarding in unexpected ways, and after you visit a new area, your list becomes a souvenir of your experiences there. Keeping regular, accurate lists of birds in your neighborhood can also be useful for local researchers. It can be interesting to compare the arrival dates and last sightings of hummingbirds and other seasonal visitors, or to note the first sighting of a new visitor to your area.

BIRD FEEDING

Many people set up bird feeders in their backyard, especially in winter. It is possible to attract specific birds by choosing the right kind of food and style of feeder. Keep your feeder stocked through late spring, because birds have a hard time finding food before the flowers bloom, seeds develop and insects hatch. Contrary to popular opinion, birds do not become dependent on feeders, nor do they subsequently forget to forage naturally. Be sure to clean your feeder and the surrounding area regularly to prevent the spread of disease.

Landscaping your property with native plants is another way of providing natural food for birds. Flocks of waxwings have a keen eye for red mountain-ash berries and hummingbirds enjoy columbine flowers. The cumulative effects of "nature-scaping" urban yards can be a significant step toward habitat conservation, especially when you consider that habitat is often lost in small amounts (a power line is cut in one area and a highway is built in another). Many good books and websites about attracting wildlife to your backyard are available.

NEST BOXES

Another popular way to attract birds is to put up nest boxes, especially for Eastern Bluebirds and Purple Martins. Not all birds will use nest boxes: only species that normally use cavities in trees are comfortable in such confined spaces. Larger nest boxes can attract kestrels, owls and cavity-nesting ducks.

CLEANING NEST BOXES AND FEEDERS

Nest boxes and feeding stations must be kept clean to prevent birds from becoming ill or spreading disease. Old nesting material may harbor a number of parasites. Once the birds have left for the season, remove the old nesting material and wash and scrub the nest box with detergent or a 10 percent bleach solution (1 part bleach to 9 parts water). You can also scald the nest box with boiling water. Rinse it well and let it dry thoroughly before you remount it.

Unclean bird feeders can become contaminated with salmonellosis and possibly other diseases. Seed feeders should be cleaned monthly; hummingbird feeders at least weekly. Any seed, fruit or suet that is moldy or spoiled must be discarded. Clean and disinfect feeding stations with a 10 percent bleach solution, scrubbing thoroughly. Rinse the feeder well and allow it to dry completely before refilling it.

Red-breasted
Merganser

Discarded seed and feces on the ground under the feeding station should also be removed.

We advise that you wear rubber gloves and a mask when cleaning nest boxes or feeders.

WEST NILE VIRUS

Since the West Nile Virus first surfaced in North America in 1999, it has caused fear and misunderstanding. Some people have become afraid of contracting the disease from birds, and some health departments have advised residents to eliminate feeding stations and birdbaths.

To date, the disease has reportedly killed 284 species of birds. Corvids (crows, jays and ravens) and raptors have been the most obvious victims because of their size, though the disease also affects some smaller species. The virus is transmitted among birds and to humans (as well as some other mammals) by mosquitoes that have bitten infected birds. Birds do not get the disease directly from other birds, and humans cannot get it from casual contact with infected birds. As well, not all mosquito species can carry the disease. According to the Centers for Disease Control and Prevention (CDC), only about 20 percent of people who are bitten and become infected will develop any symptoms at all and less than 1 percent will become severely ill.

Because mosquitoes breed in standing water, birdbaths have the potential to become mosquito breeding grounds. Birdbaths should be emptied and have the water changed at least weekly. Drippers, circulating pumps, fountains or waterfalls that keep water moving will prevent mosquitoes from laying their eggs in the water. There are also bird-friendly products available to treat water in birdbaths. Contact your local nature store or garden center for more information on these products.

ABOUT THE SPECIES ACCOUNTS

This book gives detailed accounts of 105 species of birds that can be expected in South Carolina on an annual basis. The order of the birds and their common and scientific names follow the American Ornithologists' Union's *Check-list of North American Birds* (7th edition, July 1998, and its supplements through 2005).

As well as showing the identifying features of the bird, each species account also attempts to bring the bird to life by describing its various character traits. One of the challenges of birding is that many species look different in spring and summer than they do in fall and winter. Many birds have breeding and nonbreeding plumages, and immature birds often look different from their parents. This book does not try to describe or illustrate all the different plumages of a species; instead, it tries to focus on the forms that are most likely to be seen in our area.

ID: Large illustrations point out prominent field marks that will help you tell each bird apart. The descriptions favor easily understood language instead of technical terms.

Other ID: This section lists additional identifying features. Some of the most common anatomical features of birds are pointed out in the Glossary illustration (p. 231).

Size: The average length of the bird's body from bill to tail, as well as wingspan, are given and are approximate measurements of the bird as it is seen in nature. The size is sometimes given as a range, because there is variation between individuals, or between males and females.

Voice: You will hear many birds, particularly song-birds, which may remain hidden from view. Memorable paraphrases of distinctive sounds will aid you in identifying a species by ear.

Status: A general comment, such as "common," "uncommon" or "rare," is usually sufficient to describe the relative abundance of a species. Situations are bound to vary somewhat since migratory pulses, seasonal changes and centers of activity tend to concentrate or disperse birds.

Habitat: This section describes where each species is most commonly found. Because of the freedom that flight gives them, birds can turn up in almost any type of habitat. However, they will usually be found in environments that provide the specific food, water, cover and, in some cases, nesting habitat that they need to survive.

Similar Birds: Easily confused species are illustrated for each account. If you concentrate on the most relevant field marks, the subtle differences between species can be reduced to easily identifiable traits. Even experienced birders can mistake one species for another.

Nesting: In each species account, nest location and structure, clutch size, incubation period and parental duties are discussed. A photo of the bird's egg is also provided. Remember that birding ethics discourage the disturbance of active bird nests. If you disturb a nest, you may drive off the parents during a critical period or expose defenseless young to predators.

Range Maps: The range map for each species shows the overall range of the species in an average year. Most birds will confine their annual movements to this range, although each year some birds wander beyond their traditional boundaries. The maps show breeding, summer and winter ranges, as well as migratory pathways (areas of the region where birds may appear while en route to nesting or winter habitat). The representations of the pathways do not distinguish high-use migration corridors from areas that are seldom used.

Range Map Symbols

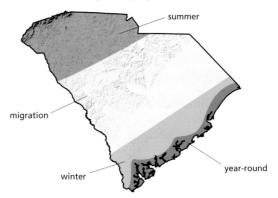

TOP BIRDING SITES

From the lowlands near the coast to the western mountains, our state can be separated into three natural regions: the Coastal Plain, Piedmont and Mountains. Each region is composed of a number of different habitats that support a wealth of wildlife.

There are hundreds of good birding areas throughout our region. The following areas have been selected to represent a broad range of bird communities and habitats, with an emphasis on accessibility.

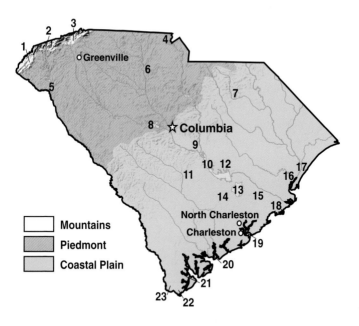

1. Oconee SP	12. Santee NWR
2. Walhalla Fish Hatchery	13. Lake Moultrie
3. Caesars Head SP	14. Francis Biedler Forest
4. Sassafrass Mountain	15. Francis Marion NF
5. Lake Hartwell	16. Brookgreen Gardens
6. Broad River Recreation Area	17. Huntington Beach SP
7. Carolina Sandhills NWR	18. Cape Romain NWR
8. Lake Murray	19. Folly Island
9. Congaree Swamp NM	20. Bear Island WMA
10. Lake Marion	21. Pinckney Island NWR
11. Orangeburg Sod Farms	22. Savannah Spoils Area
	23. Savannah NWR

NF = National Forest   SP = State Park
NM = National Monument   WMA = Wildlife Management Area
NWR = National Wildlife Refuge

Canada Goose
Branta canadensis

Previously, thousands of Canada Geese descended on South Carolina each winter, but now many birds cut short their migration to enjoy the abundant food supply found in the corn and grainfields of the Midwest. Though a few migratory geese regularly visit South Carolina each year, many of our geese are resident, nonmigratory individuals and flocks. • The Canada Goose was split into two species in 2004. The larger subspecies, which breed in the central U.S., are known as Canada Geese, whereas the smaller, arctic breeding subspecies have been renamed Cackling Geese.

Other ID: dark brown upperparts; light brown underparts; short, black tail; white undertail coverts. *In flight:* flocks fly in V-formation.
Size: *L* 3–4 ft; *W* up to 6 ft.
Voice: loud, familiar *ah-honk*.
Status: common permanent resident; numbers increase in winter at the coast and at large inland lakes as migrants return.
Habitat: lakeshores, riverbanks, ponds, farmlands and city parks.

Similar Birds

Cackling Goose

Brant

long, black neck

white "chin strap"

Nesting: usually on the ground; female builds a nest of grass and mud, lined with down; white eggs are 3½ × 2¼ in; female incubates 3–8 eggs for 25–28 days; goslings are born in early spring.

Did You Know?

Canada geese mate for life, but unlike most young birds, goslings remain with their devoted parents for nearly a year.

Look For

Pairs of Canada Geese settle down to nesting activities in April, and the first downy goslings of the year are normally seen before mid-May.

Wood Duck

Aix sponsa

A forest-dwelling duck, the Wood Duck is equipped with fairly sharp claws for perching on branches and nesting in tree cavities. Shortly after hatching, the ducklings jump out of their nest cavity, often falling 20 feet or more. Like downy balls, they bounce on landing and are seldom injured. • Female Wood Ducks often return to the same nest site year after year, especially after successfully raising a brood. Established nest sites, where the adults are familiar with potential threats, may improve the young's chance of survival.

Other ID: long tail. *Male:* glossy, green head with some white streaks; white-spotted, purplish chestnut breast; golden sides. *Female:* gray-brown upperparts; white belly.

Size: *L* 15–20 in; *W* 30 in.

Voice: *Male:* ascending *ter-wee-wee. Female:* squeaky *woo-e-e-k.*

Status: common permanent resident, but uncommon in the Mountains in winter.

Habitat: swamps, ponds, marshes and lakeshores with wooded edges.

Similar Birds

Hooded Merganser

Look For

A male duck defending his mate from other suitors will often srike the interloper with an open wing when he gets too close.

white, teardrop-shaped eye patch

crest is slicked back from crown

♀

♂

mottled brown breast is streaked with white

black and white shoulder slash

white chin and throat

Nesting: in a hollow or tree cavity; may be as high as 30 ft up; also in an artificial nest box; usually near water; cavity is lined with down; white to buff eggs are 2⅛ × 1⅝ in; female incubates 9–14 eggs for 25–35 days.

Did You Know?

Landowners with a small, treelined pond or other suitable wetland may attract a family of Wood Ducks by building a suitably sized nest box with a predator guard and lining it with sawdust. The nest box should be close to the shoreline and at least 5 feet from the ground.

Mallard
Anas platyrhynchos

Mallards can be seen year-round, often in flocks and always near open water. • After breeding, male ducks lose their elaborate plumage. The drab "eclipse" plumage helps them stay camouflaged during their flightless period. In early fall, they molt back into breeding colors. • Mallards can sleep with one eye open. The brain hemisphere on the opposite side of the open eye remains partially awake, watching for predators or other dangers, while the hemisphere opposite the closed eye is fully asleep!

Other ID: orange feet. *Male:* white "necklace"; black tail feathers curl upward. *Female:* mottled brown overall. *In flight:* dark blue speculum bordered by white.
Size: L 20–28 in; W 3 ft.
Voice: quacks; female is louder than male.
Status: common permanent resident, with numbers increasing at the coast in winter.
Habitat: lakes, wetlands, rivers, city parks, agricultural areas and sewage lagoons.

Similar Birds

Northern Shoveler

American Black Duck

glossy green head

yellow bill

orange bill
spattered
with black

♂

♀

Nesting: a grass nest is built on the ground or under a bush; creamy, grayish or greenish white eggs are 2¼ × 1⅝ in; female incubates 7–10 eggs for 26–30 days.

Did You Know?

A nesting hen generates enough body heat to make the grass around her nest grow faster. She then uses the tall grass to further conceal her precious nest.

Look For

Mallards will freely hybridize with American Black Ducks as well as domestic ducks. The resulting offspring are a confusing blend of both parental types.

Northern Pintail
Anas acuta

Its long neck and long, tapered tail put this dabbling duck in a class of its own. The elegant and graceful Northern Pintail breeds in Asia and northern Europe, as well as in North America.
• These migrants leave the state early in spring to scout out flooded agricultural fields farther north for choice nesting locations. Unfortunately, Northern Pintails usually build their nests in vulnerable areas, on exposed ground near water, a habit that has resulted in a slow decline in their population.

Other ID: *Male:* dusty gray body plumage; black and white hindquarters; long, tapering tail feathers.
Size: *Male:* L 25–30 in; W 34 in. *Female:* L 20–22 in; W 34 in.
Voice: *Male:* soft, whistling call. *Female:* rough quack.
Status: common winter resident at the coast; uncommon migrant and winter resident in the Piedmont.
Habitat: shallow wetlands, flooded fields and lake edges.

Similar Birds

Mallard
(p. 24)

Gadwall

Long-tailed Duck

chocolate brown head

mottled, light brown overall

white on breast extends up sides of slender neck

Nesting: does not nest in South Carolina; nests from the northern U.S. to the Arctic; in a small depression in vegetation; nest of grass, leaves and moss is lined with down; greenish buff eggs are 2⅛ × 1½ in; female incubates 6–12 eggs for 22–25 days.

Did You Know?

The Northern Pintail, one of the most abundant waterfowl species on the continent, migrates at night at altitudes of up to 3000 feet.

Look For

The long, pointed tail of the male Northern Pintail is easily seen in flight and points sky-ward when the bird tips up to dabble.

Bufflehead
Bucephala albeola

A Bufflehead will typically spend its entire life in North America, dividing its time between breeding grounds in the boreal forests of Canada and Alaska and winter territory primarily in marine bays and estuaries along the Atlantic and Pacific coasts. Watch for small flocks of these birds foraging near piers. • Fish, crustaceans and mollusks make up a major portion of the Bufflehead's winter diet, but in summer this duck eats large amounts of aquatic invertebrates and tubers.

Other ID: very small, rounded duck; short neck; white neck and underparts; light brown sides.
Male: dark back.
Size: *L* 13–15 in; *W* 21 in.
Voice: *Male:* growling call.
Female: harsh quack.
Status: common migrant and winter resident in the Coastal Plain; rare migrant in the Mountains.
Habitat: coastal waters; brackish and freshwater wetlands.

Similar Birds

Hooded Merganser

Common Goldeneye

white speculum

white, oval
ear patch

white
wedge

iridescent, dark
green or purple
head usually
appears black

short, gray
bill

Nesting: does not nest in South Carolina;
nests in Canada and Alaska; in a tree cavity;
often near water; pale buff to cream-colored
eggs are 2 × 1½ in; female incubates 6–12 eggs
for 28–33 days.

Did You Know?

Buffleheads are part of
the "sea duck" group.
This group features skilled
divers that can tolerate salt
water and cold climates.

Look For

Buffleheads gather where
tidal bays are constricted.
They appear to spend as
much time chasing each
other as they do diving for
mollusks such as snails.

Red-breasted Merganser

Mergus serrator

A spiky, double-pointed crest gives the Red-breasted Merganser a unique, windswept look. This medium-sized duck prefers cooler water and breeds in northern lakes where small fish are abundant, then returns to salt water, along both the Atlantic and Pacific coasts, to overwinter. Mergansers often feed in water bodies with featureless, sandy bottoms. Groups sometimes fish cooperatively, funneling fishes for easier capture. Sizable concentrations assemble on bays and in ocean coves wherever small, schooling fishes are abundant.

Other ID: *Male:* green head; black and white wing covers; red eyes. *Female:* gray-brown overall; reddish head. *In flight:* 2 white wing patches.
Size: *L* 23 in; *W* 30 in.
Voice: *Male:* catlike *yeow* during courtship and feeding.
Female: harsh *kho-kha*.
Status: common migrant and winter resident at the coast; uncommon migrant in the Piedmont at large lakes.
Habitat: coastal waters and estuaries; large freshwater lakes.

Similar Birds

Double-crested Cormorant (p. 42)

Hooded Merganser, female

Red-throated Loon

shaggy, slicked-back crest

thin, red, serrated bill

white collar

♂

light rusty breast is spotted with black

gray sides

Nesting: rare nester in South Carolina, with all records from around Charleston; on the ground, in a depression lined with plant material and down; creamy or pale green eggs are 2½ × 1¾ in; female incubates 7–12 eggs for 28–35 days.

Did You Know?

The scientific name *serrator* refers to this bird's serrated bill, which is perfect for gripping slippery fish.

Look For

The female Red-breasted Merganser has a pale, reddish brown head and lacks the white throat patch of the female Common Merganser.

Wild Turkey
Meleagris gallopavo

The Wild Turkey was once common throughout most of eastern North America, but in the early 20th century, habitat loss and overhunting took a toll on this bird. Today, efforts at restoration have reestablished the Wild Turkey in many areas of South Carolina. • This charismatic bird is the only native North American animal that has been widely domesticated. The wild ancestors of most domestic animals came from Europe. • If Congress had taken Benjamin Franklin's advice in 1782, our national emblem would be the Wild Turkey instead of the majestic Bald Eagle.

Other ID: barred, copper-colored tail. *Male:* black-tipped breast feathers. *Female:* blue-gray head; brown-tipped breast feathers.
Size: *Male:* L 3–3½ ft; W 5½ ft.
Female: L 3 ft; W 4 ft.
Voice: courting male gobbles loudly; contact call is a loud *keouk-keouk-keouk*.
Status: fairly common permanent resident; increasing.
Habitat: deciduous, mixed and riparian woodlands; occasionally eats waste grain and corn in late fall and winter.

Similar Birds

Ruffed Grouse

Look For

Eastern Wild Turkeys have brown or rusty tail tips and are slimmer than domestic turkeys, which have white tail tips.

naked,
blue-red head

dark, glossy,
iridescent body
plumage

red wattles

♂

long, central
breast tassel

Nesting: in a woodland or at a field edge; on the ground in a depression under thick cover; nest is lined with grass and leaves; brown-speckled, pale buff eggs are 2½ × 1¾ in; female incubates 10–12 eggs for up to 28 days.

Did You Know?

Early in life both male and female turkeys gobble. The females eventually outgrow this practice, leaving the males to gobble competitively for the honor of mating. Once a male has attracted a female with his gobbling call, he struts around her with his tail fanned out like a peacock.

Northern Bobwhite
Colinus virginianus

The characteristic, whistled *bob-white* call of our only native quail is heard throughout South Carolina in spring. The male's well-known call is often the only evidence of this bird's presence among the dense, tangled vegetation of its rural, woodland home. • In fall and winter, Northern Bobwhites typically travel in large family groups called coveys. With the arrival of summer, breeding pairs break away from their coveys to perform elaborate courtship rituals in preparation for another nesting season.

Other ID: mottled, brown, buff and black upperparts; white crescents and spots edged in black on chestnut brown sides and upper breast; short tail.
Size: *L* 10 in; *W* 13 in.
Voice: whistled *hoy* is given year-round. *Male:* a whistled, rising *bob-white* in spring and summer.
Status: formerly a common permanent resident; has declined dramatically.
Habitat: farmlands, open woodlands, woodland edges, grassy fencelines, road-side ditches and brushy, open country.

Similar Birds

Ruffed Grouse

Look For

Bobwhites are often found in the early succession habitats created by fire, agriculture and forestry.

buffy throat and eyebrow

broad, white eyebrow

♂

white throat

rufous breast

♀

Nesting: in a shallow depression on the ground, often concealed by vegetation or a woven, partial dome; nest is lined with grass and leaves; white to pale buff eggs are $1\frac{1}{4} \times 1$ in; pair incubates 12–16 eggs for 22–24 days.

Did You Know?

When they huddle, members of the covey all face outward, enabling the group to detect danger from any direction. When a predator approaches, the covey bursts into flight, creating a confusing flurry of activity.

Pied-billed Grebe
Podilymbus podiceps

Relatively solid bones and the ability to partially deflate its air sac allow the Pied-billed Grebe to sink below the surface of the water like a tiny submarine.

breeding

• Pied-billed Grebes are seen year-round in South Carolina, but they are most common from September to May, when solitary individuals are often seen on larger rivers and lakes, especially near the coast.

Other ID: *Breeding:* dark eye with pale ring; black ring on pale bill; black throat; white undertail coverts; pale belly.
Size: *L* 12–15 in; *W* 16 in.
Voice: loud, whooping call begins quickly, then slows down: *kuk-kuk-kuk cow cow cow cowp cowp cowp.*
Status: common statewide in migration and winter; rare in summer but some breeding has occurred in the Coastal Plain.
Habitat: ponds, marshes and backwaters with sparse emergent vegetation.

Similar Birds

American Coot
(p. 76)

Horned Grebe

brownish crown

bill lacks
black ring

dark upperparts

white chin
and throat

nonbreeding

reddish
underparts

Nesting: rare in South Carolina, usually in the
Coastal Plain; among sparse vegetation in wetlands; floating platform nest made of decaying
plants is anchored to emergent vegetation;
white to buff eggs are 1⅝ × 1¼ in; pair incubates 4–5 eggs for about 23 days.

Did You Know?

When these grebes are
frightened by an intruder,
they cover their eggs and
slide underwater, leaving a
nest that looks like nothing
more than a mat of debris.

Look For

Dark plumage, individually
webbed toes and a chicken-
like bill distinguish Pied-billed
Grebes from other water-
fowl.

Northern Gannet
Morus bassanus

The Northern Gannet, with its elegant face mask and high forehead, slices through the open ocean air with blackened wing tips. It is a pelagic bird that spends months at sea, sometimes resting on the water but rarely landing on solid earth except to nest. • This gentle-looking bird does not breed until it is at least five years of age, and it mates for life. To reestablish their bond each year, pairs affectionately dip their bills to the breast of their mate, bow, raise their wings and preen each other.

Other ID: white overall; long, narrow wings; pointed tail; black feet. *Juvenile:* variably mottled with brown and gray.
Size: L 3–3¼ ft; W 6 ft.
Voice: usually silent at sea; feeding flocks may exchange grating growls.
Status: common winter resident and migrant offshore.
Habitat: roosts and feeds in open ocean waters most of the year; often seen well offshore; regularly seen near shore during migration and in winter.

Similar Birds

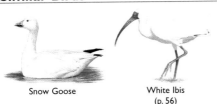

Snow Goose

White Ibis
(p. 56)

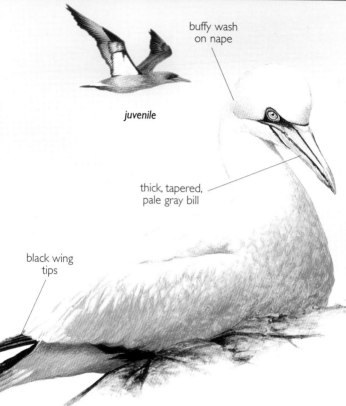

buffy wash
on nape

juvenile

thick, tapered,
pale gray bill

black wing
tips

Nesting: does not nest in South Carolina; nests on islands in the Canadian Atlantic; in a shallow hollow on a mound of material, usually seaweed, lined with feathers and other plants; dull, chalky white egg is 3¼ × 2 in; pair incubates 1 egg (rarely 2) for 43–45 days.

Did You Know?

The single egg that a pair of gannets lays is incubated under the webs of the feet, which have extra blood vessels for better temperature regulation.

Look For

Squadrons of gannets soaring at over 100 feet high will suddenly fold their wings back and simultaneously plunge headfirst into the ocean in pursuit of schooling fish.

Brown Pelican
Pelecanus occidentalis

With even wingbeats, Brown Pelicans float gracefully above the sunbathers and fishing boats along our coastline. These conspicuous waterbirds perch on beaches, rocks and pilings or course the troughs in single file. Brown Pelicans are strictly a coastal species, seldom encountered away from marine or intertidal habitats. • In the 1950s and 1960s, DDT-related reproductive failures caused Brown Pelicans to nearly disappear in South Carolina and in many areas of the southeastern U.S. Since these highly persistent pesticides were banned in the 1970s, pelican populations have recovered.

Other ID: *Nonbreeding:* white neck; yellow wash on head; pale yellowish pouch.
Size: *L* 4 ft; *W* 7 ft.
Voice: generally silent.
Status: critically imperiled; federal species of special concern; common permanent resident along the coast.
Habitat: coastal and estuarine waters, ranging over the continental shelf in some areas; visits offshore islands; roosts on protected islets, sea stacks, sandbars and piers.

Similar Birds

American White Pelican

Look For

The Brown Pelican forages by a unique plunge-dive method: it folds its wings, pulls back its head and dives headfirst into the water, trapping fish in its flexible pouch.

yellow head

dark brown
hindneck

grayish brown
body

very large bill
and red pouch

breeding

Nesting: on the ground; a scrape nest or an
elaborate platform woven from sticks and lined
with vegetation; bright, chalky white eggs are
3 × 2 in; pair incubates 2–3 eggs under footwebs
for 29–32 days; both parents care for young.

Did You Know?

In a single scoop, a pelican can trap over 3 gallons of water
and fish in its bill, which is about two to three times as much
as its stomach can hold. The Brown Pelican's diet is mostly
composed of small, surface-schooling fishes.

Double-crested Cormorant

Phalacrocorax auritus

The Double-crested Cormorant looks like a bird but smells and swims like a fish. With a long, rudder-like tail and excellent underwater vision, this slick-feathered bird has mastered the underwater world. Most waterbirds have waterproof feathers, but the structure of the Double-crested Cormorant's feathers allows water in. "Wettable" feathers make this bird less buoyant, which in turn makes it a better diver. The Double-crested Cormorant also has sealed nostrils for diving, so it must fly with its bill open.

Other ID: *Juvenile:* brown upperparts; buff throat and breast. *In flight:* rapid wingbeats; kinked neck.
Size: L 26–32 in; W 4¼ ft.
Voice: generally quiet; may issue piglike grunts or croaks.
Status: abundant at the coast in winter and in migration; common in summer at the coast, the Coastal Plain and at some large inland lakes; statewide migrant, becoming less common farther inland.
Habitat: large lakes and large, meandering rivers; lagoons and estuaries.

Similar Birds

Great Cormorant

Common Loon

Anhinga
(p. 44)

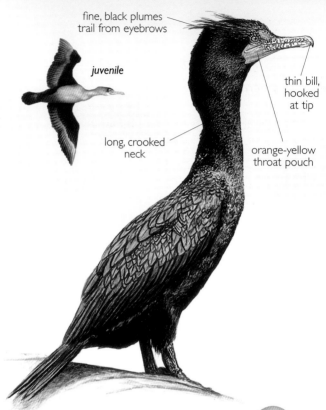

fine, black plumes
trail from eyebrows

juvenile

thin bill,
hooked
at tip

long, crooked
neck

orange-yellow
throat pouch

Nesting: nests in South Carolina at Lake Moultrie and Lake Marion; colonial; on an island or high in a tree; platform nest is made of sticks and guano; pale blue eggs are 2 × 1½ in; both sexes incubate 2–7 eggs for 25–30 days.

Did You Know?

Japanese fishermen sometimes use cormorants on leashes to catch fish. This traditional method of fishing is called *Ukai*.

Look For

Double-crested Cormorants often perch on trees or piers with their wings partially spread. Lacking oil glands, they use the wind to dry their feathers.

Anhinga
Anhinga anhinga

The Anhinga's ability to control its buoyancy gives
it a stealthy hunting technique and makes it an
ominous presence in our freshwater ponds and
canals. With dense bones and easily waterlogged
feathers, it swims almost completely submerged,
holding its curved neck just above water, often
appearing snakelike. With one quick lunge and
a stab of its long, sharp bill, the Anhinga captures
prey, which is flipped in the air and swallowed
headfirst. • Following a swim, Anhingas unfold
their silver-streaked wings to dry out their feathers
before they can fly.

Other ID: rather large waterbird. *Breeding male:*
blue-green orbital ring. *Female* and *immature:* buffy
head and neck.
Size: L 2½–3 ft; W 4 ft.
Voice: descending metallic
clicks while perched.
Status: common in summer in
the Coastal Plain, and less common
in winter; rarely in the Piedmont at
any season.
Habitat: quiet, sheltered, slowly moving
or still fresh water.

Similar Birds

Double-crested
Cormorant (p. 42)

Great Cormorant

long, curved neck

black body with silver
and white streaking

red eyes

♂

long, fanlike tail

breeding

Nesting: colonial; in a tree
above water; male brings
sticks but female builds nest;
chalky blue to white eggs are
2 × 1½ in; pair incubates 3–5 eggs
for 25–29 days.

Did You Know?

The Anhinga is the sole
New World member of
the Darters (Anhingidae),
a family of birds related to
cormorants but restricted
to fresh water.

Look For

Flocks of Anhingas are often
seen soaring high above on
thermals.

Great Blue Heron
Ardea herodias

The long-legged Great Blue Heron has a stealthy, often motionless hunting strategy. It waits for a fish or frog to approach, spears the prey with its bill, then flips its catch into the air and swallows it whole. Herons usually hunt near water, but they also stalk rodents in fields and meadows. • Great Blue Herons settle in communal treetop nests called rookeries. Nesting herons are sensitive to human disturbance, so observe this bird's behavior from a distance.

Other ID: blue-gray overall; long, dark legs. *Breeding:* richer colors; plumes streak from crown and throat. *In flight:* neck folds back over shoulders; black upperwing tips; legs trail behind body; slow, steady wingbeats.

Size: *L* 4¼–4½ ft; *W* 6 ft.

Voice: quiet away from the nest; occasional harsh *frahnk frahnk frahnk* during takeoff.

Status: common year-round but less common inland in winter; more abundant at the coast and in the Coastal Plain in winter; breeds in the Coastal Plain and sparingly in the lower Piedmont.

Habitat: forages along edges of rivers, lakes and marshes; also in fields and wet meadows.

Similar Birds

Little Blue Heron

Tricolored Heron

Sandhill Crane

breeding

black plumes above eye

breeding

long, curving neck with black markings on throat

straight, yellow bill

chestnut brown thighs

Nesting: colonial; adds to its stick platform nest over years; nest width can reach 4 ft; pale bluish green eggs are 2½ × 1¾ in; pair incubates 4–7 eggs for approximately 28 days.

Did You Know?

The Great Blue Heron is the tallest of all herons and egrets in North America.

Look For

In flight, the Great Blue Heron folds its neck back over its shoulders in an S-shape. Similar-looking cranes stretch their necks out when flying.

Great Egret
Ardea alba

The plumes of Great Egrets and Snowy Egrets were widely used to decorate hats in the early 20th century. An ounce of egret feathers cost as much as $32—more than an ounce of gold at that time—and, as a result, egret populations began to disappear. Some of the first conservation legislation in North America was enacted to outlaw the hunting of Great Egrets. This bird became the symbol for the National Audubon Society, one of our country's oldest conservation organizations.

Other ID: all-white plumage. *In flight:* neck folds back over shoulders; legs extend backward.
Size: L 3–3½ ft; W 4 ft.
Voice: rapid, low-pitched, loud *cuk-cuk-cuk*.
Status: common permanent resident in the Coastal Plain; less common in winter; uncommon post-breeding wanderer in the Piedmont.
Habitat: marshes, open riverbanks, irrigation canals and lakeshores.

Similar Birds

Snowy Egret
(p. 50)

Cattle Egret

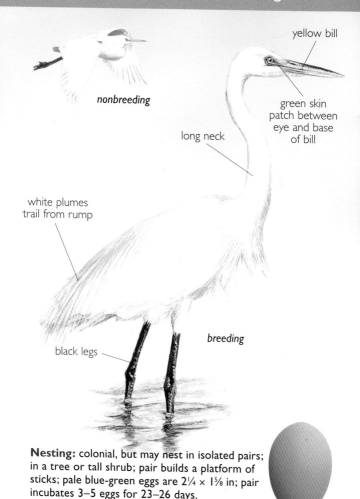

nonbreeding

yellow bill

green skin patch between eye and base of bill

long neck

white plumes trail from rump

black legs

breeding

Nesting: colonial, but may nest in isolated pairs; in a tree or tall shrub; pair builds a platform of sticks; pale blue-green eggs are 2¼ × 1⅝ in; pair incubates 3–5 eggs for 23–26 days.

Did You Know?

Great Egrets are named for their impressive breeding plumes, or "aigrettes," which can grow up to 4½ feet long!

Look For

A crafty Great Egret will sometimes feed near a White Ibis, taking advantage of prey that the ibis frightens to the surface but cannot reach.

Snowy Egret

Egretta thula

Looking as if it stepped in a can of yellow paint, the dainty Snowy Egret flaunts famously yellow feet on black legs. Come breeding season, the egret's lores and feet turn a deeper orange, and long plumes extend from its neck and back. It was perhaps the most sought-after target for the plume trade because of the abundance of fine aigrettes on its body. Like other wading birds, Snowy Egrets teetered on the brink of extirpation in South Carolina by the early 1900s. Their populations have recovered dramatically, and they now occur beyond their historical range limits in North America.

Other ID: a medium-sized, all-white wading bird.
Size: L 22–26 in; W 3½ ft.
Voice: generally silent away from colonies.
Status: common permanent resident near the coast; uncommon migrant inland.
Habitat: edges of marshes, rivers, lakes and ponds; flooded agricultural fields.

Similar Birds

Great Egret (p. 48)

Cattle Egret

Little Blue Heron, immature

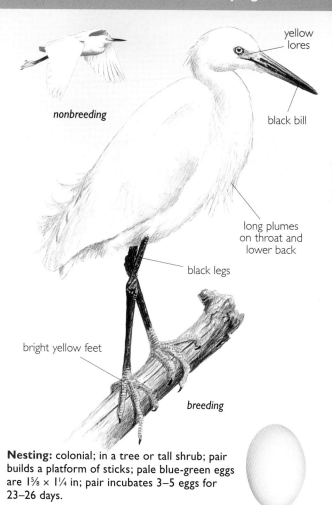

nonbreeding

yellow lores

black bill

long plumes on throat and lower back

black legs

bright yellow feet

breeding

Nesting: colonial; in a tree or tall shrub; pair builds a platform of sticks; pale blue-green eggs are 1⅝ × 1¼ in; pair incubates 3–5 eggs for 23–26 days.

Did You Know?

These birds feed by actively chasing prey or by poking their bright yellow feet in the muck of shallow wetlands, flushing out prey.

Look For

Foraging egrets sometimes extend their wings over open water to create shade, which provides better visibility and attracts fish seeking shelter from the sun.

Green Heron
Butorides virescens

Sentinel of the marshes, the ever-vigilant Green Heron sits hunched on a shaded branch at the water's edge. This crow-sized heron stalks frogs and small fish lurking in the weedy shallows, then stabs the prey with its bill. • Unlike most herons, the Green Heron nests singly rather than communally, though it can sometimes be found in loose colonies. Whereas some of this heron's habitat has been lost to wetland drainage or channelization in the southern states, the building of farm ponds or reservoirs has created habitat in other areas.

Other ID: stocky body; relatively short, yellow-green legs; bill is dark above and greenish below; short tail. *Breeding male:* bright orange legs.
Size: L 15–22 in; W 26 in.
Voice: generally silent; alarm or flight call is a loud *kowp, kyow* or *skow;* aggression call is a harsh *raah.*
Status: common summer resident in the coastal plain, becoming scarcer in summer inland; locally rare winter resident at the coast.
Habitat: marshes, lakes and streams with dense shoreline or emergent vegetation.

Similar Birds

Black-crowned
Night-Heron (p. 54)

Yellow-crowned
Night-Heron

Least Bittern

dark, iridescent back

green-black crown

chestnut face and neck

Nesting: nests singly or in small, loose groups; platform nest is in a tree or shrub, usually very close to water; pale blue-green eggs are 1½ × 1⅛ in; pair incubates 3–5 eggs for 19–21 days.

Did You Know?

Butorides species are often seen baiting fish to the surface by dropping small bits of debris such as twigs, vegetation or feathers.

Look For

The Green Heron often appears bluish or black; the iridescent green shine on the back and outer wings is only visible in certain light.

Black-crowned Night-Heron

Nycticorax nycticorax

When dusk's long shadows shroud the marshes, Black-crowned Night-Herons arrive to hunt in the marshy waters. These herons crouch motionless, using their large, light-sensitive eyes to spot prey lurking in the shallows. • Black-crowned Night-Herons breed throughout much of the United States. Watch for them in summer, between dawn and dusk, as they fly from nesting colonies to feeding areas and back. They are most common along the coast, especially at Huntington Beach.

Other ID: black back; white foreneck and underparts; gray neck and wings; dull yellow legs; stout, black bill. *Immature:* streaked with brown and white.

Size: *L* 23–26 in; *W* 3½ ft.

Voice: deep, guttural *quark* or *wok*.

Status: common coastal permanent resident; rare inland above the lower Coastal Plain.

Habitat: shallow cattail and bulrush marshes, lakeshores and along slow rivers.

Similar Birds

Yellow-crowned
Night-Heron

Green Heron
(p. 52)

American Bittern

feet protrude only slightly beyond tail

immature

black cap with 2 white plumes

large, red eyes

white cheek

breeding

stocky body

Nesting: colonial; in a tree or shrub; male gathers nest material; female builds a loose nest platform of twigs and sticks and lines it with finer materials; pale green eggs are $2\frac{1}{4} \times 1$ in; pair incubates 3–4 eggs for 21–26 days.

Did You Know?

Nycticorax, meaning "night raven," refers to this bird's distinctive nighttime calls.

Look For

To distinguish Black-crowned Night-Herons in flight, look at their feet, which are shorter than the feet of other herons and project only partially beyond the tail.

White Ibis
Eudocimus albus

White Ibises congregate on our coastline, often close to heronries, picking slowly through the mud for tasty crabs or crayfish. These birds can be cunning thieves, stealing food from other wading birds and, if the opportunity arises, even snatching nest-building material from others in their own colony. • Breeding success is heavily dependent on the rainy season of late April or May when freshwater pools form, a necessity for feeding the salt-sensitive young. • This bird can be found in Francis Biedler Forest.

Other ID: *Breeding:* tip of bill becomes dark. *Immature:* brown-gray head, neck and uppersides; white rump and belly. *In flight:* small, dark wing tips; outstretched neck.
Size: L 22 in; W 3 ft.
Voice: mostly silent; throaty alarm or flight call: *hungk-hungk-hungk.*
Status: common permanent resident along the coast and in the Coastal Plain; uncommon migrant inland.
Habitat: shallow water; estuaries, flooded fields and swamps.

Similar Birds

Glossy Ibis   Long-billed Curlew   Snowy Egret
(p. 50)

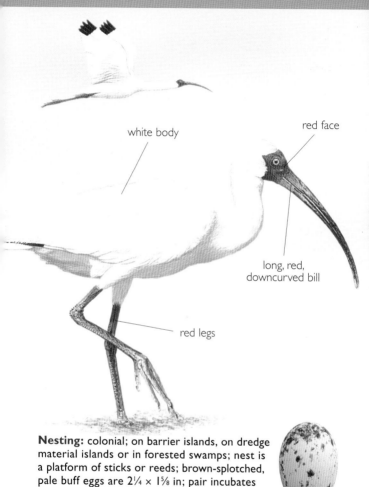

white body

red face

long, red,
downcurved bill

red legs

Nesting: colonial; on barrier islands, on dredge
material islands or in forested swamps; nest is
a platform of sticks or reeds; brown-splotched,
pale buff eggs are $2\frac{1}{4} \times 1\frac{5}{8}$ in; pair incubates
2–4 eggs for 21–22 days.

Did You Know?

Larger birds often pirate
food from ibises, and
smaller birds frequently
follow close behind,
snatching stirred up
invertebrates.

Look For

These highly nomadic birds
commute between nesting
and feeding areas in long,
cohesive lines or V-patterns
that may reach a mile long.

Wood Stork

Mycteria americana

The impressive Wood Stork inhabits the Southeast's cypress swamps and marshes and is the only stork found regularly in North America. • In order to feed its large young over the prolonged nesting period, a Wood Stork needs receding water levels 6 to 10 inches deep to concentrate prey in pools. Since this stork has specific habitat needs, it is considered an indicator species. Monitoring indicator species allows scientists to judge the overall state of an ecosystem without untangling its intricate details. • The Wood Stork is endangered, but populations seem to be stable.

Other ID: *In flight:* often soars in flocks.
Size: *L* 3–3½ ft; *W* 5–5½ ft.
Voice: generally silent.
Status: critically imperiled; federally endangered; fairly common in the lower Coastal Plain south toward the Georgia border in summer; locally present in winter; rare post-breeding wanderer to the lower Piedmont.
Habitat: freshwater ponds and marshes, cypress swamps and ponds; flooded agricultural fields.

Similar Birds

American White Pelican

Snow Goose

unfeathered blackish head and neck

black flight feathers and tail

large, dark, slightly down-curved bill

Nesting: colonial; nests high in a cypress; male brings sticks to the female to build a stick platform lined with leaves and twigs; white eggs are 2⅝ × 1¾ in; pair incubates 2–5 eggs for 28–32 days.

Did You Know?

The legend that storks bring forth human babies is likely based on the White Stork *(Ciconia ciconia)*, a bird that still nests on European rooftops.

Look For

Their large wing surface allows Wood Storks to soar to great heights, often in large, swirling flocks. Unlike most other wading birds, Wood Storks fly with their necks extended outward.

Turkey Vulture
Cathartes aura

The genus name *Cathartes* means "cleanser" and refers to this bird's affinity for carrion. The red, featherless head may appear grotesque, but this adaptation allows the bird to stay relatively clean while feeding on messy carcasses. A vulture's bill and feet are much less powerful than those of eagles, hawks or falcons, which kill live prey. • No other birds use updrafts and thermals in flight as well as the Turkey Vulture. Pilots have reported seeing vultures soaring at 20,000 feet.

Other ID: *Immature:* gray head. *In flight:* head appears small; rocks from side to side when soaring.
Size: *L* 25–31 in; *W* 5½–6 ft.
Voice: generally silent; occasionally produces a hiss or grunt if threatened.
Status: common permanent resident; numbers increase during migration and winter.
Habitat: usually flies over open country, shorelines or roads; rarely over forests.

Similar Birds

Black Vulture

Golden Eagle

Bald Eagle
(p. 66)

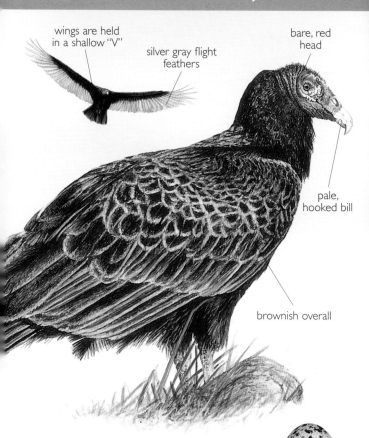

wings are held in a shallow "V"

silver gray flight feathers

bare, red head

pale, hooked bill

brownish overall

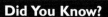

Nesting: in a cave, crevice, log or among boulders; uses no nest material; dull white or creamy, brown-spotted eggs are 2¾ × 2 in; pair incubates 2 eggs for up to 41 days.

Did You Know?

Despite their similarities to birds of prey, vultures are considered most closely related to storks.

Look For

Turkey Vultures live and sleep together in large trees, or "roosts." Some roost sites are over a century old and have been used by the same family of vultures for generations.

Osprey

Pandion haliaetus

The Osprey is almost always found near water. Its dark eye line blocks the glare of the sun on the water, enabling the bird to spot fish near the water's surface. While hunting, the Osprey hovers in the air before hurling itself into a dramatic headfirst dive. An instant before striking the water, it rights itself and thrusts its feet forward to grasp its quarry. The Osprey has specialized feet for gripping slippery prey—two toes point forward, two point backward and all are covered with sharp spines.

Other ID: yellow eyes; pale crown; dark "necklace" may or may not be present. *In flight:* long wings are held in a shallow "M"; dark "wrist" patches; brown and white tail bands.
Size: *L* 22–25 in; *W* 5½–6 ft.
Voice: series of melodious ascending whistles: *chewk-chewk-chewk;* also a familiar *kip-kip-kip.*
Status: common breeder in the Coastal Plain and on large Piedmont lakes; fairly common migrant statewide; uncommon at the coast in winter.
Habitat: lakes and slow-flowing rivers and streams; estuaries and bays in migration.

Similar Birds

Bald Eagle
(p. 66)

Look For

Ospreys build bulky nests on high, artificial structures such as communication towers and utility poles, or on buoys and channel markers over water.

dark eye line

gray bill

♀

♂

gray feet

long wings
extend past tail

Nesting: on a treetop or artificial structure, usually near water; massive stick nest is reused annually; yellowish, brown-blotched eggs are 2⅜ × 1¾ in; pair incubates 2–4 eggs for 38 days.

Did You Know?

The Osprey is one of the most widely distributed birds in the world—it is found on every continent except Antarctica. In the mid-1900s it went through a drastic population decline in North America related to the harmful effects of the pesticide DDT, but it has since recovered rapidly.

Mississippi Kite
Ictinia mississippiensis

Most often seen in flight, the Mississippi Kite floats buoyantly above the Coastal Plain, flapping lazily but rarely gliding. It feeds on flying insects such as dragonflies, cicadas, beetles and grasshoppers, which are plucked out of the air with the bird's feet and eaten while in flight. Occasionally, acrobatic aerial pursuits end in the successful capture of vertebrates, including bats, swallows and swifts.

• Mississippi Kites were traditionally restricted to the southern states, but their breeding range seems to be expanding northward, with sightings now occurring to southern New England.

Other ID: *In flight:* long wings and tail; gray over-all; male has white inner wing patches; short outer-most primary feather.
Size: *L* 14 in; *W* 3 ft.
Voice: generally silent; alarm call: *kee-kew, kew-kew.*
Status: federal species of special concern, but secure in South Carolina; common in summer in the Coastal Plain and farther inland along major river corridors.
Habitat: deciduous or mixed wood-lands; riparian areas.

Similar Birds

Northern Harrier, male

Peregrine Falcon

pale head

dark gray back and wings

dark gray underparts

black tail

Nesting: in a tall tree; pair constructs a flimsy stick platform lined with leaves; bluish white eggs are 1⅝ × 1⅜ in; pair incubates 2 eggs for 30–32 days.

Did You Know?

This sociable bird relies on protective, tall trees for nesting and nighttime roosting but requires adjacent areas of open country for hunting.

Look For

In flight, the Mississippi Kite's long, pointed wings resemble a falcon, but its short outermost primary (or first wing feather) is distinctive.

Bald Eagle
Haliaeetus leucocephalus

This majestic sea eagle hunts mostly fish and is often found near water. While soaring hundreds of feet high, an eagle can spot fish swimming underwater and small rodents scurrying through the grass. It also scavenges carrion and steals food from other birds. • Pairs perform dramatic aerial displays. The most impressive display involves the two birds flying to a great height, locking talons and then tumbling perilously toward the earth, breaking away just before they risk crashing into the ground.

Other ID: *1st year:* dark overall; dark bill; some white in underwings. *2nd year:* dark bib; white in underwings. *3rd year:* yellow at base of bill; yellow eyes. *4th year:* light head with dark facial streak; variable pale and dark plumage; yellow bill; paler eyes.
Size: L 30–43 in; W 5½–8 ft.
Voice: thin, weak squeal or gull-like cackle: *kleek-kik-kik-kik* or *kah-kah-kah.*
Status: imperiled statewide; federally endangered; becoming a fairly common breeder in the Coastal Plain and at large inland lakes; fairly common migrant statewide and in winter at the coast and at large lakes.
Habitat: large lakes and rivers.

Similar Birds

Golden Eagle

Osprey
(p. 62)

white head

yellow bill

immature

white tail

yellow feet

Nesting: in a tree; usually, but not always, near water; huge stick nest is often reused for many years; white eggs are 2¾ × 2⅛ in; pair incubates 1–3 eggs for 34–36 days.

Did You Know?

The Bald Eagle, a symbol of freedom, longevity and strength, became the emblem of the United States in 1782.

Look For

Bald Eagles mate for life and renew pair bonds by adding sticks to their nests, which can be up to 15 feet in diameter (the largest of any North American bird).

Red-shouldered Hawk

Buteo lineatus

The Red-shouldered Hawk likes wetter habitats than its close relatives. It nests in mature trees, usually around river bottoms and in lowland tracts of woods alongside creeks. As spring approaches and pair bonds are formed, this normally quiet hawk utters loud, shrieking *key-ah* calls. • Most buteos have broad wings and fan-shaped tails for soaring, whereas accipters (woodland hawks), have shorter, more rounded wings and long, rudderlike tails for high-speed maneuvers.

Other ID: dark brown upperparts; reddish under-wing linings; narrow, white bars on dark tail; reddish undertail coverts.
Size: *L* 19 in; *W* 3½ ft.
Voice: repeated series of high *key-ah* notes.
Status: uncommon permanent resident in the Piedmont, becoming more common in the Coastal Plain; uncommon migrant in the Mountains.
Habitat: mature deciduous and mixed forests, wooded riparian areas, swampy woodlands and large, mature woodlots.

Similar Birds

Broad-winged Hawk

Red-tailed Hawk
(p. 70)

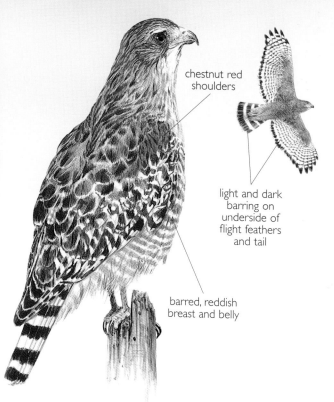

chestnut red
shoulders

light and dark
barring on
underside of
flight feathers
and tail

barred, reddish
breast and belly

Nesting: pair assembles a bulky stick nest in a deciduous tree; nest is often reused; darkly blotched, bluish white eggs are 2¼ × 1⅝ in; female incubates 2–4 eggs for about 33 days.

Did You Know?

Red-shouldered Hawks remain faithful to productive nesting sites, returning yearly, as long as the sites are left undisturbed.

Look For

In flight, the Red-shouldered Hawk has several narrow, white tail bars, while the Broad-winged Hawk has one prominent, white tail bar.

Red-tailed Hawk
Buteo jamaicensis

Take an afternoon drive through the country and look for Red-tailed Hawks soaring above the fields. Red-tails are the most common hawks in South Carolina, especially in winter. • In warm weather, these hawks use thermals and updrafts to soar. The pockets of rising air provide substantial lift, which allows migrating hawks to fly for almost 2 miles without flapping their wings. • The Red-tailed Hawk's impressive, piercing call is often misleadingly paired with the image of an eagle in TV commercials and movies.

Other ID: brown eyes. *In flight:* dark "shoulder" patches; light underwing flight feathers with faint barring; dark leading edge on underside of wing; fan-shaped tail.
Size: *Male: L* 18–23 in; W 4–5 ft. *Female: L* 20–25 in; W 4–5 ft.
Voice: powerful, descending scream: *keeearrrr.*
Status: common permanent resident; numbers increase in winter.
Habitat: open country with some trees; also roadsides or woodlots.

Similar Birds

Broad-winged Hawk

Red-shouldered Hawk
(p. 68)

juvenile

dark upperparts
with some white
highlights

dark brown
band of
streaks across
belly

red tail

Nesting: in woodlands adjacent
to open habitat; bulky stick nest is
enlarged each year; brown-blotched,
whitish eggs are $2\frac{3}{8} \times 1\frac{7}{8}$ in; pair incubates
2–4 eggs for 28–35 days.

Did You Know?

Over the Red-tailed
Hawk's entire range,
there are 16 subspecies,
and most but not all bear
the characteristic red tail.

Look For

On cooler days, resident
Red-tails perch on exposed
tree limbs, fence posts or
utility poles to scan for prey.

American Kestrel
Falco sparverius

The colorful American Kestrel, formerly known as the "Sparrow Hawk," is a common and widespread falcon, not shy of human activity and adaptable to habitat change. This small falcon has benefited from the grassy rights-of-way created by interstate highways, which provide habitat for grasshoppers and other small prey. Watch for this robin-sized bird along rural roadways, perched on poles and telephone wires or hovering over agricultural fields, foraging for insects and small mammals.

ID: lightly spotted underparts. *In flight:* frequently hovers; buoyant, indirect flight style.
Size: L 7½–8 in; W 20–24 in.
Voice: usually silent; loud, often repeated, shrill *killy-killy-killy* when excited; female's voice is lower pitched.
Status: fairly common perma-nent resident in the Coastal Plain and Piedmont; fairly common migrant statewide; numbers increase in winter.
Habitat: open fields, riparian woodlands, woodlots, forest edges, bogs, roadside ditches, grassy highway medians, grasslands and croplands.

Similar Birds

Merlin

Sharp-shinned Hawk

Peregrine Falcon

long, rusty tail ♂

2 distinctive facial stripes

rusty wings and breast streaking

blue-gray crown with rusty cap

♀

rusty barring on back

blue-gray wings

♂

Nesting: in a tree cavity; may use a nest box; white to buff, brown-spotted eggs are 1½ × 1⅛ in; mostly the female incubates 4–6 eggs for 29–30 days; both adults raise the young.

Did You Know?

No stranger to captivity, the American Kestrel was the first falcon to reproduce by artificial insemination.

Look For

The American Kestrel repeatedly lifts its tail while perched to scout below for prey.

Purple Gallinule

Porphyrio martinica

Wearing almost every color of the rainbow, this unique bird is one of the treasures of the southeastern swamps and a "must-see" for visitors to South Carolina. Watch for Purple Gallinules at Savannah River National Wildlife Refuge, swimming through the shallows, bobbing their heads with great zeal. • Purple Gallinules prefer quiet freshwater marshes thick with lily pads, alligator flag and other plants, which they agilely navigate, propelled by their large feet and long toes.

Other ID: slender body shape; white undertail coverts. *Juvenile:* bronzy upperparts; buffy brown head and breast; dusky bill and frontal shield.
Size: *L* 12–14 in; *W* 22 in.
Voice: various henlike clucks, cackles or high-pitched notes.
Status: common summer resident at Savannah River NWR; uncommon elsewhere near the coast.
Habitat: freshwater marshes, ponds and lakes with floating vegetation and dense cover.

Similar Birds

American Coot
(p. 76)

Common Moorhen

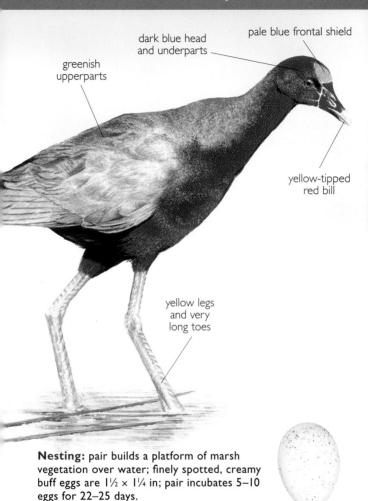

greenish upperparts

dark blue head and underparts

pale blue frontal shield

yellow-tipped red bill

yellow legs and very long toes

Nesting: pair builds a platform of marsh vegetation over water; finely spotted, creamy buff eggs are 1½ × 1¼ in; pair incubates 5–10 eggs for 22–25 days.

Did You Know?

When a gallinule takes over incubation duties, it often offers its mate a leaf or piece of grass, which is added to the nest as the birds change over.

Look For

The closely related Purple Gallinule, Common Moorhen and American Coot all flick their conspicuous, white undertail coverts when they walk.

American Coot
Fulica americana

American Coots resemble ducks but are actually more closely related to rails and gallinules. They are extremely abundant on our lakes, reservoirs and wetlands from September to May, when they form dense flocks as protection from Bald Eagles and other large, predatory birds. • With feet that have individually webbed toes, the coot is adapted to diving, but it isn't afraid to snatch a meal from another skilled diver. The American Coot eats aquatic vegetation as well as a variety of invertebrates and fish, and it sometimes even grazes on land.

Other ID: red eyes; long, yellow-green legs; lobed toes; small, white marks on tail.
Size: *L* 13–16 in; *W* 24 in.
Voice: calls frequently in summer, day and night: *kuk-kuk-kuk-kuk-kuk*; also croaks and grunts.
Status: common winter visitor; rare breeder in the Coastal Plain.
Habitat: shallow marshes, ponds and wetlands with open water and emergent vegetation; also sewage lagoons.

Similar Birds

Common Moorhen

Purple Gallinule
(p. 74)

reddish spot on
white forehead
shield

white, chicken-
like bill with
dark ring
around tip

gray-black overall

Nesting: in emergent vegetation; pair builds
floating nest of cattails and grass; buffy white,
brown-spotted eggs are 2 × 1⅜ in; pair incubates
8–12 eggs for 21–25 days; raises 2 broods per
year.

Did You Know?

American Coots are the
most widespread and
abundant members of
the rail family in North
America.

Look For

Though it resembles a duck,
an American Coot bobs its
head while swimming or
walking, lacks fully webbed
feet and has a narrower bill
that extends up the forehead.

Black-bellied Plover
Pluvialis squatarola

Black-bellied Plovers may be seen along the coast in winter, roosting in tight flocks or running along the mudflats when the tide goes out. These large plovers forage with a robinlike run-and-stop technique as they search for small invertebrates, and they frequently pause to lift their heads for a reassuring scan of their surroundings. They are usually found in coastal habitats but are equally comfortable foraging inland near fresh water. Watch for small flocks flashing their bold white wing stripes as they fly low over the water's surface.

Other ID: *Breeding:* white stripe leads from crown down collar, neck and sides of breast; black face, breast, belly and flanks; white undertail coverts; mottled, black and white back.
Size: *L* 10½–13 in; *W* 29 in.
Voice: rich, plaintive, 3-syllable whistle: *pee-oo-ee.*
Status: common winter resident in the Coastal Plain; uncommon migrant in the lower Piedmont.
Habitat: coastal mudflats and beaches; plowed fields, sod farms and meadows; the edges of lakeshores and reservoirs.

Similar Birds

American Golden-Plover   Western Sandpiper

nonbreeding

black "wing pits"

mottled, gray-brown upperparts

short, black bill

lightly streaked, pale underparts

long, black legs

nonbreeding

Nesting: does not nest in South Carolina; nests in the Arctic, on the ground; scrape nest is lined with moss or lichen; darkly marked, buff, grayish or brownish eggs are 2 × 1½ in; both adults, but mainly male, incubate 4 eggs for 27 days.

Did You Know?

Most plovers have three toes, but the Black-bellied Plover has a fourth toe higher on its leg, like most sandpipers.

Look For

The Black-bellied Plover often forages with migrating and wintering flocks of Killdeers, especially in farm fields.

Killdeer
Charadrius vociferus

The Killdeer is a gifted actor, well known for its "broken wing" distraction display. When an intruder wanders too close to its nest, the Killdeer greets the interloper with piteous cries while dragging a wing and stumbling about as if injured. Most predators take the bait and follow, and once the Killdeer has lured the predator far away from its nest, it miraculously recovers from the injury and flies off with a loud call.

Other ID: brown head; white neck band; brown back and upperwings; white underparts; rufous rump. *Immature:* downy; only 1 breast band.
Size: *L* 9–11 in; *W* 24 in.
Voice: loud, distinctive *kill-dee kill-dee kill-deer;* variations include *deer-deer.*
Status: common permanent resident; more common in migration and winter.
Habitat: open areas, such as fields, lakeshores, sandy beaches, mudflats, gravel streambeds, wet meadows and grasslands.

Similar Birds

Semipalmated Plover   Piping Plover   Wilson's Plover

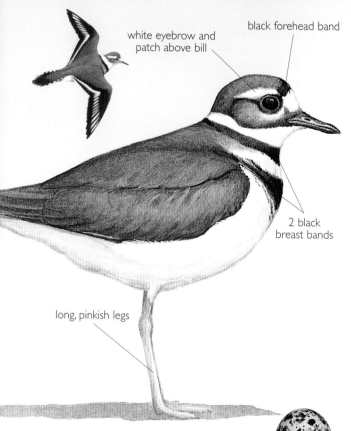

white eyebrow and patch above bill

black forehead band

2 black breast bands

long, pinkish legs

Nesting: on open ground, in a shallow, usually unlined depression; heavily marked, creamy buff eggs are 1⅜ × 1⅛ in; pair incubates 4 eggs for 24–28 days; may raise 2 broods.

Did You Know?

In spring, you might hear a European Starling imitate the vocal Killdeer's call.

Look For

The Killdeer has adapted well to urbanization. It finds golf courses, farms, fields, gravel rooftops and abandoned industrial areas as much to its liking as shorelines.

American Oystercatcher

Haematopus palliatus

One of the few birds with a bill sturdy enough to pry open a mollusk shell, the American Oystercatcher eats a variety of shellfish, including oysters, clams and mussels. This large shorebird uses its bill to pound open mussel shells, shovel and leverage clams up through the sand and pry limpets away from rocks. It usually forages silently and alone, but it issues loud whistles as it flies between mudflats and shellfish beds. Look for it at Huntington Beach State Park.

Other ID: stocky build; short tail. *In flight:* bold white wing stripe and rump patch.
Size: *L* 18½ in; *W* 32 in.
Voice: call is a loud *wheet!*, often given in series during flight.
Status: common permanent resident along the coast.
Habitat: coastal marine habitats, including saltwater marshes, sandy beaches and tidal mudflats; will nest on dredge spoil islands.

Look For

During the summer breeding season, watch for amusing courtship displays. These birds issue loud "piping" calls while they run along together side by side, bobbing their heads up and down. They may also take to the air, still calling and maintaining proximity.

brown back

black head
and neck

long, orange-
red bill

white underparts

Nesting: scrape nest in sandy depression may be lined with dead plants, shells or pebbles; yellowish to brown, boldly marked eggs are 2¼ × 1½ in; pair incubates 2–4 eggs for 24–27 days; may mate for life.

Did You Know?

American Oystercatchers may form a breeding trio, made of two females and one male. Together, the group tends up to two nests and feeds the brood for the first weeks. Downy, newly hatched young are able to leave the nest a day or two after they are born. Chicks will pick at small insects almost immediately, but adults supply most food for the first two months.

Greater Yellowlegs
Tringa melanoleuca

The Greater Yellowlegs and Lesser Yellowlegs
(*T. flavipes*) are medium-sized sandpipers with
very similar plumages; they also share the yellow
legs and feet that give them their English name.
Both species differ subtly, and a solitary
Greater Yellowlegs is difficult to identify until
it flushes and utters its distinctive three peeps (the
Lesser Yellowlegs peeps only once or twice). As its
name suggests, the Greater Yellowlegs is the larger
species, and it has a slightly upturned, longer bill
that is about 1½ times the width of its head.

Other ID: plain plumage; bill may have gray base.
Nonbreeding: upperparts less marked; dusky breast;
pale underparts. *Breeding:* streaked breast; flanks
barred with black. *In flight:* tail is finely barred;
white rump.
Size: L 13–15 in; W 28 in.
Voice: call is a loud whistled
tew-tew-tew.
Status: common migrant statewide; uncommon winter resident in
the Coastal Plain.
Habitat: any type of shallow wetland,
whether freshwater, brackish or salt;
flooded agricultural fields.

Similar Birds

Lesser Yellowlegs

Solitary Sandpiper

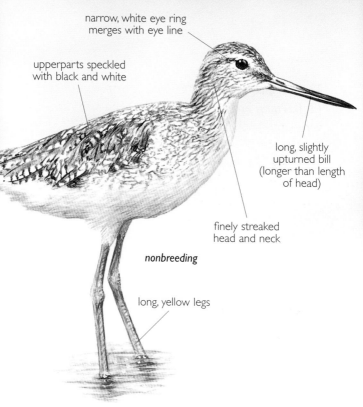

narrow, white eye ring merges with eye line

upperparts speckled with black and white

long, slightly upturned bill (longer than length of head)

finely streaked head and neck

nonbreeding

long, yellow legs

Nesting: does not breed in South Carolina; nests in Alaska and northern Canada; on the ground, near water; nest is a depression lined with leaves, moss and grass; darkly marked, pale creamy buff eggs are 2 × 1½ in; female incubates 4 eggs for 23 days.

Did You Know?

At the first sign of danger, the Greater Yellowlegs utters its loud, distinctive, trisyllabic *tew-tew-tew* call to warn other shorebirds.

Look For

Shorebirds, including the Greater Yellowlegs, often stand or hop around mud-flats on one leg, a stance that conserves body heat.

Willet
Catoptrophorus semipalmatus

Though plain and inconspicuous at rest, Willets are striking in flight, revealing a bold black and white wing pattern. They are commonly found in flocks of dozens of individuals, often towering over the other shorebirds and uttering loud *pill-will-willet* calls. • There are two distinct subspecies of the Willet, a western and an eastern variety. The eastern race, *semipalmatus,* rarely ventures far from the Atlantic Coast, whereas the western race, *inornatus,* breeds in the Great Plains and winters on the Pacific Coast.

Other ID: *Nonbreeding:* plain gray upperparts; blackish bill; whitish underparts. *In flight:* bold white wing stripe on black wings.
Size: *L* 14–16 in; *W* 26 in.
Voice: call is a loud, rolling *pill-will willet.*
Status: common permanent resident at the coast; rare wanderer inland.
Habitat: brackish and saline marshes, and beaches; rarely at flooded agricultural fields inland.

Similar Birds

Marbled Godwit

Greater Yellowlegs
(p. 84)

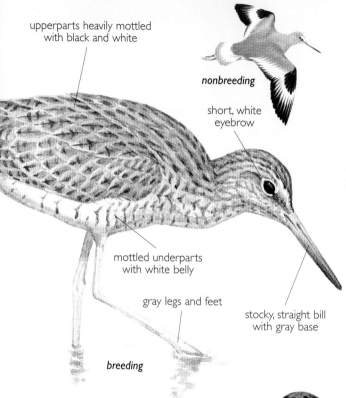

upperparts heavily mottled with black and white

nonbreeding

short, white eyebrow

mottled underparts with white belly

gray legs and feet

stocky, straight bill with gray base

breeding

Nesting: scrapes out a depression in the sand or mud; may line it with vegetation; heavily spotted, olive or buff eggs are 2¼ × 1½ in; female incubates 4 eggs for 22 days.

Did You Know?

The Latin name *catoptrophorus* means "mirror bearing," referring to this bird's white wing patches; *semipalmatus* means "partially webbed feet."

Look For

When feeding, Willets often spread out, but when one bird takes flight, the entire flock calls to each other and follows suit.

Spotted Sandpiper
Actitis macularius

The female Spotted Sandpiper, unlike most other female birds, lays her eggs and leaves the male to tend the clutch. Each summer, the female can lay up to four clutches and is capable of producing 20 eggs. After completion of her clutches, she may depart from the breeding grounds and begin her migration, leaving egg incubation and chick raising to the male. Only about one percent of birds display this unusual breeding strategy known as "polyandry."

Other ID: teeters almost continuously. *Nonbreeding* and *immature:* pure white breast and throat; brown bill; dull yellow legs. *In flight:* flies close to the water's surface with very rapid, shallow wingbeats.
Size: L 7–8 in; W 15 in.
Voice: sharp, crisp *eat-wheat, eat-wheat, wheat-wheat-wheat-wheat*.
Status: uncommon migrant at the coast; more common inland on lakes and rivers; rare breeder; very rare in winter.
Habitat: shorelines, gravel beaches, drainage ditches, swamps and sewage lagoons; occasionally seen in cultivated fields.

Similar Birds

Solitary Sandpiper

Dunlin

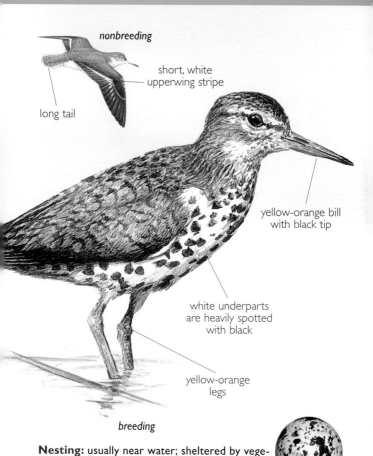

nonbreeding

short, white
upperwing stripe

long tail

yellow-orange bill
with black tip

white underparts
are heavily spotted
with black

yellow-orange
legs

breeding

Nesting: usually near water; sheltered by vegetation; shallow scrape is lined with grass; darkly blotched, creamy buff eggs are 1¼ × 1 in; male incubates the 4–5 eggs for 20–24 days.

Did You Know?

Sandpipers have four toes: three pointing forward and one pointing backward. Most plovers, such as the Killdeer, have only three toes.

Look For

Spotted Sandpipers bob their tails constantly on shore and fly with rapid, shallow, stiff-winged strokes.

Ruddy Turnstone

Arenaria interpres

Boldly marked Ruddy Turnstones are well-named shorebirds with painted faces and eye-catching, black and red backs. They are named for their habit of using their bill to flip over pebbles, shells and washed-up vegetation to expose hidden invertebrates. They also use their slender, slightly upturned bill to dig through the sand and to hammer open mollusk shells. • Ruddy Turnstones are truly long-distance migrants. They breed in the Arctic and overwinter along the coasts, from the United States to the tip of South America; they are also found in Europe and northwestern Africa.

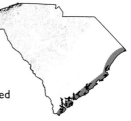

Other ID: reddish legs and feet. *Nonbreeding:* mottled brown upperparts; brown head with black markings. *In flight:* white wedge on rump; white wing stripes; white tail with broad, black band.
Size: *L* 9½ in; *W* 21 in.
Voice: a low-pitched rattle.
Status: common at the coast year-round; less common in summer; very rare inland during migration.
Habitat: sandy or rocky beaches, estuaries and oyster bars; also flooded agricultural fields during migration.

Look For?

Small flocks actively walk along the beach or roost on washed-up vegetation, relying on their plumage for camouflage. When they take flight, they exhibit strong flight on long, pointed, narrow wings with conspicuous white wing stripes.

white head with bold black markings

short, black, slightly upturned bill

black and rufous upperparts

nonbreeding

♂

bold black "bib"

breeding

Nesting: does not breed in South Carolina; nests in the Arctic; on the ground on an island or shoreline near water; scrape nest has little or no lining; pale bluish or green, speckled eggs are 1½ × 1¼ in; pair incubates 4 eggs for 21–23 days.

Did You Know?

The Ruddy Turnstone has a varied diet and will eat whatever food is most available, including insects, worms, the eggs of other birds and handouts from humans, such as leftover french fries or even coconut meat. On its arctic breeding grounds this charming little bird can even be found in bushes, eating berries.

Sanderling
Calidris alba

This cosmopolitan shorebird graces sandy shorelines around the world. It skips and plays in the waves, snatching up aquatic invertebrates before they are swept back into the water. On shores where wave action is limited, it resorts to probing mudflats for a meal of mollusks and insects. It rests from its zigzag dance along a beach to stand with one leg tucked up, a posture that conserves body heat. Sanderlings often seek the company of roosting sandpipers or plovers and turnstones for increased protection from predators.

Other ID: *Breeding:* rufous head, neck and underparts; mottled gray upperparts; white patch around bill. *Nonbreeding:* black shoulder patch (often concealed). *In flight:* dark leading edge of wing.
Size: L 7–8½ in; W 17 in.
Voice: flight call is a sharp *kip* or *plick*.
Status: common at the coast year-round; less common in summer; rare migrant inland in fall.
Habitat: sandy and muddy shorelines, cobble and pebble beaches, spits, lakeshores, marshes and reservoirs.

Similar Birds

Least Sandpiper   Semipalmated Sandpiper   Western Sandpiper

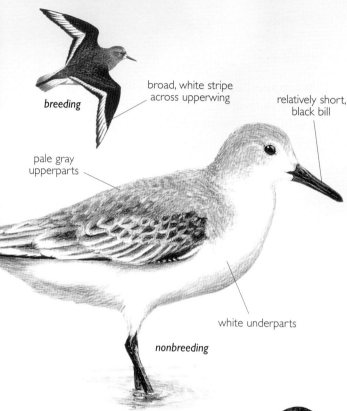

breeding

broad, white stripe
across upperwing

relatively short,
black bill

pale gray
upperparts

white underparts

nonbreeding

Nesting: does not nest in South Carolina; nests
in the Arctic, on the ground; cup nest is lined
with leaves; olive eggs, blotched with brown
or purple are 1½ × 1 in; both sexes incubate
3–4 eggs for 23–24 days.

Did You Know?

The Sanderling is wide-
spread, breeding across
the Arctic and wintering
on whatever continent
it chooses, excluding
Antarctica.

Look For

Sanderlings in pale nonbreeding plumage reflect a ghostly
glow as they forage at night
on moonlit beaches.

American Woodcock

Scolopax minor

The unusual American Woodcock is a solitary, forest-dwelling shorebird that lives in moist woodlands, avoids saline habitats and remains hidden during daylight hours. • During the breeding season, the male American Woodcock performs a dazzling courtship display. At dawn or dusk, he struts around a brushy clearing while uttering a series of loud *peent* notes. He then launches into the air, twittering upward in a circular flight until, with wings partly folded, he plummets to the ground in a zigzag pattern, chirping at every turn, and returns to where he started. The twittering sounds are made by air rushing past his outer primary flight feathers.

Other ID: stocky body with boldly patterned upperparts. *In flight:* rounded wings.
Size: L 11 in; W 18 in.
Voice: call is a nasal *peent*.
Status: fairly common year-round; more common in late fall as migrants from farther north join residents.
Habitat: moist woodlands and hammocks adjacent to grassy clearings or fields.

Similar Birds

Wilson's Snipe

Short-billed Dowitcher

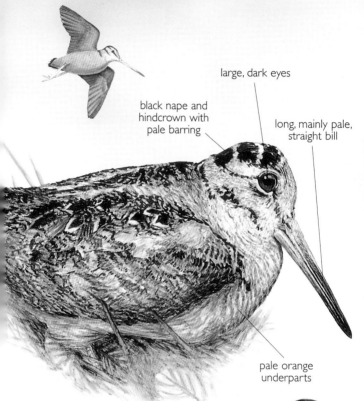

large, dark eyes

black nape and
hindcrown with
pale barring

long, mainly pale,
straight bill

pale orange
underparts

Nesting: on the ground; female digs a scrape and
lines it with dried leaves; brown-blotched, creamy
buff eggs are 1½ × 1¼ in; female incubates 4 eggs
for 20–22 days and tends the young.

Did You Know?

The clearing of forests
and draining of woodland
swamps has degraded
large tracts of woodcock
habitat, resulting in population declines.

Look For

Watch for woodcocks at
twilight from January to
April, when males perform
their aerial courtship display
over wetlands across the
state.

Laughing Gull

Larus atricilla

Laughing Gulls were nearly extirpated from the Atlantic Coast in the late 19th century, when egg collecting was popular and feathers for women's hats were in high demand. East Coast populations have gradually recovered, and Laughing Gulls are once again common along our coastline. They are frequently seen loitering in parking lots, around beaches or following ferries, as they keep a sharp eye out for human leftovers. • When you hear this bird's call, you will understand why it is named the Laughing Gull.

Other ID: *Nonbreeding:* white head with some pale gray bands; black bill. *Immature:* variable plumage; brown to gray and white overall.
Size: L 15–17 in; W 3 ft.
Voice: loud, high-pitched, laughing call: *ha-ha-ha-ha-ha-ha.*
Status: common to abundant year-round at the coast, scarce inland; more abundant in migration and winter.
Habitat: primarily coastal in bays and estuaries, salt marshes and sandy beaches; occasionally inland shores, streams, agricultural lands or landfills.

Similar Birds

Bonaparte's Gull   Forster's Tern

nonbreeding

broken, white eye ring

black head

red bill

breeding

Nesting: colonial nester; on dry islands, sandy coastal beaches or salt marshes; builds a cup nest of marsh vegetation on the ground; brown, splotched eggs are 2¼ × 1½ in; both parents incubate 3 eggs for 22–27 days.

Did You Know?

Nesting colonies on small offshore islands are vulnerable to spring storms and high tides that flood shoreline nests.

Look For

The Latin name *atricilla* refers to a black band present only on the tails of immature birds.

Ring-billed Gull

Larus delawarensis

Few people can claim that they have never seen this common and widespread gull. Highly tolerant of humans, Ring-billed Gulls are part of our everyday lives, scavenging our litter and fouling our parks. These omnivorous gulls will eat almost anything and will swarm parks, beaches, golf courses and fast-food parking lots looking for food handouts, making pests of themselves. However, few species have adjusted to human development as well as the Ring-billed Gull, which is something to appreciate.

Other ID: *In flight:* black wing tips with a few white spots.
Size: *L* 18–20-in; *W* 4 ft.
Voice: high-pitched *kakakaka-akakaka;* also a low, laughing *yook-yook-yook.*
Status: abundant winter resident at the coast and on large inland lakes; common migrant statewide.
Habitat: *Breeding:* bare, rocky and shrubby islands and sewage ponds. *In migration* and *winter:* lakes, rivers, landfills, golf courses, fields and parks.

Similar Birds

Herring Gull

Look For

Adult Ring-billed Gulls have yellow legs and a yellow bill surrounded by a black ring, whereas adult Herring Gulls have pink legs and a red spot on their bill.

nonbreeding

yellow eyes

yellow bill with black ring around tip

mottled head

pale gray mantle

white underparts

nonbreeding

yellow legs

Nesting: does not nest in South Carolina; nests in the northern U.S. and Canada; colonial; in a shallow scrape on the ground lined with grass, debris and small sticks; brown-blotched, gray to olive eggs are 2⅜ × 1⅝ in; pair incubates 2–4 eggs for 23–28 days.

Did You Know?

In chaotic nesting colonies, adult Ring-billed Gulls can recognize the calls of their own chicks. Once the chicks are five days old, they can distinguish the calls of their parents from neighboring adults.

Royal Tern

Sterna maxima

nonbreeding

Female Royal Terns lay a single egg (or occasionally two) amid a tightly packed colony of up to 10,000 nests. Both adults take responsibility for incubating their treasure through hot, sun-drenched days, cool coastal nights and brutal summer storms. Most of the eggs in the colony hatch within a few days of each other, turning the beach colony into a raucous muddle of commotion. • Look for this tern at Savannah Spoils Area.

Other ID: *Nonbreeding:* narrow black band on head. *In flight:* deeply forked tail; thick, dark wedge on tips of upperwings.
Size: *L* 20 in; *W* 3½ ft.
Voice: bleating call is a high-pitched *kee-er;* also gives a whistling *turreee.*
Status: formerly a common breeder along the coast but is declining; more common during migration.
Habitat: coastal habitats, including sandy beaches, estuaries, saltwater marshes, islands, bays and lagoons.

Similar Birds

Caspian Tern   Forster's Tern   Common Tern

black cap is frayed
at back of head

long, orange bill

breeding

legs usually black but can
be orange in juveniles

Nesting: loss of nesting sites may threaten
birds in the near future; colony nester; usually
on sandy ground; nest is a shallow depression
lined sparsely with vegetation; heavily marked,
ivory eggs are 2½ × 1¾ in; pair incubates 1–2
eggs for 20–25 days.

Did You Know?

Because colonies usually
grow from the center
outward, the eggs in the
centre of the colony gen-
erally hatch first.

Look For

During the breeding season,
the male Royal Tern per-
forms spiraling aerial flights,
then struts in front of the
female with offerings of fish.

Black Skimmer
Rynchops niger

nonbreeding

The Black Skimmer is the only bird in North America with a lower mandible that is longer than its upper mandible. The skimmer plows its scooplike lower mandible just below the water's surface feeling for fish, then slams its upper mandible down, clamping the slippery prey securely within its bill. • Unmistakable Black Skimmers propel themselves through the air on long, swept-back wings, flying low over shallow water.

Other ID: *Nonbreeding:* white collar and duller upperparts. *Immature:* dull, mottled brown upperparts.
Size: *L* 18 in; *W* 3½ ft.
Voice: call is a series of yapping notes.
Status: species of special concern; uncommon at the immediate coast; very rare at large inland lakes after storms.
Habitat: coastal marine habitats including estuaries, lagoons, sheltered bays and inlets.

Look For

Black Skimmers may feed at any time of the day or night, but they usually forage most actively at low tide and 2 hours before high tide.

long, thick, red bill
with black tip
(lower mandible
longer than upper
mandible)

black upperparts

white underparts

breeding

Nesting: colony nester; on beaches, sandy islands and rarely on gravel roofs; nest is a shallow scraped depression in sand; boldly blotched, white eggs are 1¾ × 1½ in; mainly female incubates 3–4 eggs for 21–23 days.

Did You Know?

At hatching, the mandibles of a baby Black Skimmer's bill are equal in length. As the bird matures, the lower mandible grows at a faster rate than the upper mandible.

Rock Pigeon
Columba livia

Rock Pigeons are familiar to almost all city-dwellers. These colorful, acrobatic, seed-eating birds frequent parks, town squares, railroad yards and factory sites. Their tolerance of humans has made them a source of entertainment, as well as a pest. • This pigeon is likely a descendant of a Eurasian bird that was first domesticated in about 4500 BC. The Rock Pigeon was introduced to North America in the 17th century by settlers.

Other ID: usually has white rump and orange feet. *In flight:* holds wings in a deep "V" while gliding.
Size: *L* 12–13 in; *W* 28 in (male is usually larger).
Voice: soft, cooing *coorrr-coorrr-coorrr.*
Status: abundant year-round in urban areas; less common in rural areas.
Habitat: urban areas, railroad yards and agricultural areas.

Similar Birds

Mourning Dove
(p. 106)

Look For

No other "wild" bird varies as much in coloration, a result of semi-domestication and extensive inbreeding over time.

overall color is highly variable (iridescent blue-gray, red, white or tan)

white cere

Nesting: in a barn or on a cliff, bridge or tower; in a flimsy nest of sticks, grass and other vegetation; glossy white eggs are 1½ × 1⅛ in; pair incubates 2 eggs for 16–19 days; may raise broods year-round.

Did You Know?

Most of our understanding of bird migration, endocrinology, color genetics and sensory perception comes from experiments involving Rock Pigeons, the most studied birds in the world.

Mourning Dove
Zenaida macroura

The Mourning Dove's soft cooing, which filters through broken woodlands and suburban parks, is often confused with the sound of a hooting owl. Beginning birders who track down the source of the calls are often surprised to find the stream-lined silhouette of a perched dove. • This popular game animal is common throughout South Carolina and is one of the most abundant native birds in North America. Its numbers and range have increased since human development has created more open habitats and food sources, such as waste grain and bird feeders.

Other ID: buffy, gray-brown plumage; small head; dark bill; sleek body; dull red legs.
Size: L 11–13 in; W 18 in.
Voice: mournful, soft, slow *oh-woe-woe-woe*.
Status: common permanent resident.
Habitat: open and riparian woodlands, forest edges, agricultural and suburban areas, open parks.

Similar Birds

Rock Pigeon
(p. 104)

Black-billed Cuckoo

pale blue eye ring

dark, shiny patch below ear

black spots on upperwing

pale rosy underparts

long, white-trimmed, tapering tail

Nesting: in a shrub or tree; occasionally on the ground; nest is a fragile, shallow platform of twigs; white eggs are 1⅛ × ⅞ in; pair incubates 2 eggs for 14 days.

Did You Know?

The Mourning Dove raises up to six broods each year—more than any other native bird.

Look For

When this bird bursts into flight, its wings clap above and below its body. It also often produces a whistling sound as it flies at high speed.

Yellow-billed Cuckoo
Coccyzus americanus

Large tracts of hardwood forest with plenty of clearings provide valuable habitat for the Yellow-billed Cuckoo, a bird that is declining over much of its range and has already disappeared in some states. The cuckoo's habitat is also steadily disappearing as waterways are altered or dammed.
• The cuckoo skillfully negotiates its tangled home within impenetrable, deciduous undergrowth in silence, relying on obscurity for survival. Then, for a short period during nesting, the male cuckoo tempts fate by issuing a barrage of loud, rhythmic courtship calls.

Other ID: olive brown upperparts; white underparts; long tail with large, white spots on underside.
Size: L 11–13 in; W 18 in.
Voice: long series of deep, hollow *kuks*, slowing near the end: *kuk-kuk-kuk-kuk kuk kop kow kowlp kowlp.*
Status: common breeder and migrant.
Habitat: semi-open deciduous habitats; dense tangles and thickets; sometimes woodlots.

Similar Birds

Black-billed Cuckoo

Mourning Dove
(p. 106)

yellow eye ring

rufous tinge on
primaries

mainly yellow,
downcurved bill
with black upper
ridge

Nesting: on a low horizontal branch in a
deciduous shrub or small tree; flimsy platform
nest of twigs is lined with grass; pale bluish green
eggs are 1¼ × ⅞ in; pair incubates 3–4 eggs for
9–11 days.

Did You Know?

The Yellow-billed Cuckoo,
or "Rain Crow," has a
propensity for calling on
dark, cloudy days and a
reputation for predicting
rainstorms.

Look For

Yellow-billed Cuckoos produce more young when out-
breaks of cicadas or tent
caterpillars provide an abundant food supply.

Eastern Screech-Owl
Megascops asio

red morph

The diminutive Eastern Screech-Owl is a year-round resident of deciduous woodlands, but its presence is rarely detected—most screech-owls sleep away the daylight hours. • The noise of a mobbing horde of chickadees or a squawking gang of Blue Jays can alert you to an owl's presence during the day. Smaller birds that mob a screech-owl often do so after losing a family member during the night. • Eastern Screech-Owls are the only owls in South Carolina to show two color morphs: both red and gray morphs occur here. Very rarely, an intermediate brown morph also occurs.

Other ID: pale grayish bill.
Size: *L* 8–9 in; *W* 20–22 in.
Voice: horselike "whinny" that rises and falls.
Status: common permanent resident.
Habitat: mature deciduous forests, open deciduous and riparian woodlands, orchards and shade trees with natural cavities.

Similar Birds

Northern Saw-whet Owl

Barred Owl

short "ear" tufts

yellow eyes

dark breast streaking

gray morph

Nesting: in an unlined natural cavity or artificial nest box; white eggs are 1½ × 1¼ in; female incubates 4–5 eggs for about 26 days; male brings food to the female during incubation.

Did You Know?

The Eastern Screech-Owl has one of the most varied diets of any owl and will capture small animals, earthworms, insects and even fish.

Look For

These owls respond readily to whistled imitations of their calls, and sometimes several owls will appear to investigate the fraudulent perpetrator.

Great Horned Owl
Bubo virginianus

This highly adaptable and superbly camouflaged hunter has sharp hearing and powerful vision that allow it to hunt at night. It will swoop down from a perch onto almost any small creature that moves. The Great Horned Owl is the only consistent predator of skunks, likely because it has a poor sense of smell. • Great Horned Owls begin their courtship as early as December, and by January or February the females are already incubating their eggs.

Other ID: overall plumage varies from light gray to dark brown; heavily mottled, gray, brown and black upperparts; yellow eyes; white chin.
Size: L 18–25 in; W 3–5 ft.
Voice: breeding call is 4–6 deep hoots: *hoo-hoo-hoooo hoo-hoo* or *Who's awake? Me too;* female gives lower-pitched hoots.
Status: common permanent resident.
Habitat: fragmented forests, fields, riparian woodlands, suburban parks and wooded edges of landfills.

Similar Birds

Long-eared Owl

Look For

Owls regurgitate pellets that contain the indigestible parts of their prey. You can find these pellets, which are generally clean and dry, under frequently used perches.

tall, widely spaced "ear" tufts form a triangle with beak

rusty orange facial disc is outlined in black

fine, horizontal barring on breast

Nesting: in another bird's abandoned stick nest or in a tree cavity; adds little or no nest material; dull whitish eggs are 2¼ × 1⅞ in; mostly the female incubates 2–3 eggs for 28–35 days.

Did You Know?

An owl has specially designed feathers on its wings to reduce noise. The leading edge of the flight feathers is fringed rather than smooth, which interrupts airflow over the wing and allows the owl to fly noiselessly.

Chuck-will's-widow
Caprimulgus carolinensis

At dusk, the Chuck-will's-widow patrols the evening skies for insects while endlessly whistling its own name. Tiny, stiff hairs called "vibrissa" encircle the Chuck-will's-widow's bill and funnel prey into its large mouth as it flies. This bird's yawning gape allows it to capture flying insects of all sizes. Occasionally, the Chuck-will's-widow will even take a small bird! • This perfectly camouflaged bird is virtually undetectable during the day, roosting on a horizontal tree limb or sitting among scattered leaves on the forest floor.

Other ID: long, rounded tail. *Male:* inner edges of the outer tail feathers are white. *Gray morph:* plain gray crown; dark spots on overall gray body.
Size: *L* 12 in; *W* 26 in.
Voice: 3 loud whistling notes often paraphrased as *chuck-will's-widow.*
Status: common breeder in the Coastal Plain and Piedmont.
Habitat: riparian woodlands, swamp edges and deciduous and pine woodlands.

Similar Birds

Whip-poor-will

Common Nighthawk

rufous morph

wings are long
and pointed

mottled, brown
and buff body
with an overall
reddish tinge

rufous morph

pale brown to
buff throat

Nesting: on bare ground; no nest is built; heavily blotched, creamy white eggs are 1⅜ × 1 in; female incubates 2 eggs for about 21 days and raises young alone.

Did You Know?

Members of the nightjar family can eat thousands of insects a day.

Look For

The eyes of nightjars mirror light, so watching for reflected points of orange or red light can be useful when trying to find these birds.

Chimney Swift

Chaetura pelagica

Chimney Swifts are the "frequent fliers" of the bird world—they feed, drink, bathe, collect nest material and even mate while they fly! They spend much of their time darting through the skies catching insects. • Chimney Swifts have small, weak legs and cannot take flight again if they land on the ground. For this reason, swifts usually cling to vertical surfaces with their strong claws.

Other ID: brown overall; slim body. *In flight:* rapid wingbeats; boomerang-shaped profile; erratic flight pattern.
Size: L 5–5½ in; W 12–13 in.
Voice: call is a rapid *chitter-chitter-chitter,* given in flight; also gives a rapid series of staccato *chip* notes.
Status: common breeder; very common migrant in September.
Habitat: forages above cities and towns; roosts and nests in chimneys; may nest in tree cavities in more remote areas.

Similar Birds

Northern Rough-winged Swallow

Bank Swallow

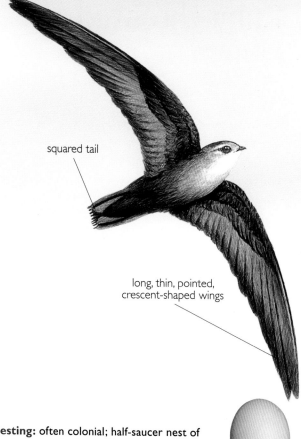

squared tail

long, thin, pointed,
crescent-shaped wings

Nesting: often colonial; half-saucer nest of
short, dead twigs is attached to a vertical wall;
white eggs are ¾ × ½ in; pair incubates 4–5 eggs
for 19–21 days.

Did You Know?

Migrating Chimney Swifts
may fly as high as 10,000
feet—above this altitude
aircraft are required to
carry oxygen.

Look For

In early evenings during
migration, Chimney Swifts
are often seen in high numbers swirling above large, old
chimneys before they enter
to roost for the night.

Ruby-throated Hummingbird

Archilochus colubris

Ruby-throated Hummingbirds feed on sweet, energy-rich flower nectar and pollinate flowers in the process. You can attract hummingbirds to your backyard with a red nectar feeder filled with a sugarwater solution (red food coloring is both unnecessary and harmful to the birds) or with native, nectar-producing flowers such as honey-suckle or bee balm.

Other ID: thin, needlelike bill; pale underparts. *Female:* green-gold crown and back; white under-parts. *Nonbreeding male:* dark brown to black throat. *Immature:* similar to female.

Size: L 3½–4 in; W 4–4½ in.

Voice: a loud *chick* and other high squeaks; soft buzzing of the wings while in flight.

Status: common breeder and abundant fall migrant.

Habitat: open, mixed woodlands, wetlands, orchards, tree-lined meadows, flower gardens and backyards with trees and feeders.

Similar Birds

Rufous Hummingbird

Look For

Vagrants of some other hummingbird species from the West Coast occasionally visit the state in winter after the Ruby-throats have gone.

fine, dark streaking on white throat

♀

iridescent, green back

♂

black chin with ruby red throat

dark tail with white tips

breeding

Nesting: on a horizontal tree limb; tiny, deep cup nest of plant down and fibers is held together with spider silk; lichens and leaves are pasted on the exterior walls; white eggs are ½ x ⅜ in; female incubates 2 eggs for 13–16 days.

Did You Know?

Weighing about as much as a nickel, a hummingbird can briefly reach speeds of up to 60 miles per hour. In straight-ahead flight, hummingbirds beat their wings up to 80 times per second, and their hearts can beat up to 1200 times per minute! Also, very few birds share a hummingbird's ability to fly vertically and in reverse.

Belted Kingfisher
Ceryle alcyon

Perched on a bare branch over a productive pool, the Belted Kingfisher utters a scratchy, rattling call. Then, with little regard for its scruffy hairdo, the "king of the fishers" plunges headfirst into the water, snatching a fish or a frog. Back on land, the kingfisher flips its prey into the air and swallows it headfirst. Similar to owls, kingfishers regurgitate the indigestible portion of their food as pellets, which can be found beneath favorite perches.

• Nestlings have closed eyes and are featherless for the first week, but after five days they are able to swallow small fish whole.

Other ID: bluish upperparts; long, small, white patch near eye; straight bill; short legs; white underwings.

Size: *L* 11–14 in; *W* 20–21 in.

Voice: fast, repetitive, cackling rattle, like a teacup shaking on a saucer.

Status: common permanent resident.

Habitat: rivers, large streams, lakes, marshes and beaver ponds, especially near exposed soil banks, gravel pits or bluffs.

Similar Birds

Blue Jay
(p. 144)

Look For

With an extra red band across her belly, the female kingfisher is more colorful than her mate.

shaggy crest

white collar

blue-gray
breast
band

♀

♂

rust-colored
belt may be
incomplete

Nesting: in a cavity at the end of an earth
burrow; no nest material added; glossy white
eggs are 1⅜ × 1 in; pair incubates 6–7 eggs for
22–24 days.

Did You Know?

Kingfisher pairs nest on sandy banks, taking turns digging a
tunnel with their sturdy bills and claws. Nest burrows may
measure up to 6 feet long and are often found near water.
Once the young are at least five days old, the parents return
to the nest regularly with small fingerling fish.

Red-headed Woodpecker

Melanerpes erythrocephalus

Red-heads were once common throughout their range, but their numbers have declined dramatically over the past century. Since the introduction of the European Starling, Red-headed Woodpeckers have been largely outcompeted for nesting cavities. • These birds are frequent traffic fatalities, often struck by vehicles when they dart from their perches and over roadways to catch flying insects.

Other ID: *Juvenile:* dark back, wings and tail; slight brown streaking on white underparts.
Size: *L* 9–9½ in; *W* 17 in.
Voice: loud series of *kweer* or *kwrring* notes; also drums softly in short bursts.
Status: federal species of special concern; uncommon permanent resident, except in the Mountains; more common in the Coastal Plain.
Habitat: open deciduous woodlands (especially oak woodlands), urban parks, river edges and roadsides with groves of scattered trees.

Similar Birds

Red-bellied
Woodpecker

Yellow-bellied
Sapsucker

bright red head

black back and wings

large, white patch

white lower back

juvenile

brown head

Nesting: male excavates a nest cavity in a dead tree or limb; white eggs are 1 × ¾ in; pair incubates 4–5 eggs for 12–13 days; pair feeds the young.

Did You Know?

The Red-headed Woodpecker is one of only four woodpecker species that regularly cache food.

Look For

The forested bottomlands, swamps and semi-open habitats of South Carolina are favorite haunts of this charismatic bird.

Downy Woodpecker

Picoides pubescens

A bird feeder well stocked with peanut butter and black oil sunflower seeds may attract a pair of Downy Woodpeckers to your backyard. These approachable little birds are more tolerant of human activity than most other species, and they visit feeders more often than the larger, more aggressive Hairy Woodpeckers *(P. villosus)*. • Like other woodpeckers, the Downy has evolved special features to help cushion the shock of repeated hammering, including a strong bill and neck muscles, a flexible, reinforced skull and a brain that is tightly packed in its protective cranium.

Other ID: black eye line and crown; white patch on back; white belly. *Male:* small, red patch on back of head. *Female:* no red patch.
Size: *L* 6–7 in; *W* 12 in.
Voice: long, unbroken trill; calls are a sharp *pik* or *ki-ki-ki* or whiny *queek queek*.
Status: common permanent resident.
Habitat: any wooded environment, especially deciduous and mixed forests and areas with tall, deciduous shrubs.

Similar Birds

Hairy Woodpecker

Yellow-bellied Sapsucker

Red-cockaded Woodpecker

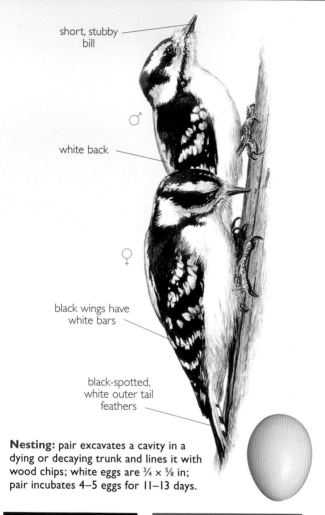

short, stubby bill

♂

white back

♀

black wings have white bars

black-spotted, white outer tail feathers

Nesting: pair excavates a cavity in a dying or decaying trunk and lines it with wood chips; white eggs are ¾ × ⅝ in; pair incubates 4–5 eggs for 11–13 days.

Did You Know?

Woodpeckers have feathered nostrils, which filter out the sawdust produced by hammering.

Look For

The Downy Woodpecker uses its small bill to probe tiny crevices for invertebrates and wood-boring grubs.

Northern Flicker

Colaptes auratus

Instead of boring holes in trees, the Northern Flicker scours the ground in search of invertebrates, particularly ants. With robinlike hops, it investigates anthills, grassy meadows and forest clearings. • Flickers often bathe in dusty depressions. The dust particles absorb oils and bacteria that can harm the birds' feathers. To clean themselves even more thoroughly, flickers squash ants and preen themselves with the remains. Ants contain formic acid, which kills small parasites on the birds' skin and feathers.

Other ID: brownish to buff face; gray crown.
Male: black "mustache" stripe; yellow underwings and undertail. *Female:* no "mustache."
Size: *L* 12–13 in; *W* 20 in.
Voice: loud, "laughing," rapid *kick-kick-kick-kick-kick-kick; woika-woika-woika* issued during courtship.
Status: common permanent resident; very common in migration and winter.
Habitat: *Breeding:* open woodlands and forest edges, fields, meadows, beaver ponds and other wetlands. *In migration* and *winter:* coastal vegetation, offshore islands and urban gardens.

Similar Birds

Red-bellied
Woodpecker

Yellow-bellied
Sapsucker

red nape crescent

black "bib"

black-spotted, buff to whitish underparts

brown, black-barred back and wings

♂

♀

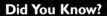

"Yellow-shafted Flicker"

Nesting: pair excavates a cavity in a dying or decaying trunk and lines it with wood chips; may also use a nest box; white eggs are 1⅛ × ⅞ in; pair incubates 5–8 eggs for 11–16 days.

Did You Know?

The very long tongue of a woodpecker wraps around twin structures in the skull and is stored like a measuring tape in its case.

Look For

Many woodpeckers have zygodactyl feet—two toes point forward and two point back—which allows them to move vertically up and down tree trunks.

Pileated Woodpecker
Dryocopus pileatus

The Pileated Woodpecker, with its flaming red crest, chisel-like bill and commanding size, requires 100 acres of mature forest as a home territory. In South Carolina, the patchwork of woodlots and small towns limits the availability of continuous habitat, requiring this woodpecker to show itself more. • A pair of woodpeckers will spend up to six weeks excavating a large nest cavity in a dead or decaying tree. Wood Ducks, kestrels, owls and even flying squirrels frequently nest in abandoned Pileated Woodpecker cavities.

Other ID: predominantly black; yellow eyes; white chin. *Male:* red "mustache." *Female:* no red "mustache"; gray-brown forehead.
Size: L 16–17 in; W 28–29 in.
Voice: loud, fast, rolling *woika-woika-woika-woika;* long series of *kuk* notes; loud, resonant drumming.
Status: fairly common permanent resident, less common in the Piedmont.
Habitat: extensive tracts of mature forests; also riparian woodlands or woodlots in suburban and agricultural areas.

Similar Birds

Red-headed
Woodpecker (p.-122)

Red-bellied
Woodpecker

flaming red crest
extends farther on male

♂

stout,
dark bill

♀

white stripe
runs from bill
to shoulder

white
wing lining

Nesting: pair excavates a cavity in a dying or decaying trunk and lines it with wood chips; white eggs are 1¼ × 1 in; pair incubates 4 eggs for 1–18 days.

Did You Know?

A woodpecker's bill becomes shorter as the bird ages, so juvenile birds have slightly longer bills than adults.

Look For

Foraging Pileated Woodpeckers leave large, rectangular cavities up to 12 inches long, usually in the trunks of trees.

Eastern Wood-Pewee
Contopus virens

Our most common and widespread woodland flycatcher, the Eastern Wood-Pewee breeds statewide in South Carolina. The male is readily detected by his plaintive, whistled *pee-ah-wee pee-oh* song, which is repeated all day long and even late into the evening throughout summer. • Many insects have evolved defense mechanisms to avert potential predators such as the Eastern Wood-Pewee and its flycatching relatives. Some flying insects are camouflaged, while others are distasteful or poisonous and flaunt their foul nature with vivid colors.

Other ID: slender body; olive gray to olive brown upperparts; whitish throat; gray breast and sides.
Size: L 6–6½ in; W 10 in.
Voice: song is a clear, slow, plaintive *pee-ah-wee*, with the 2nd note lower, followed by a downslurred *pee-oh*.
Status: fairly common breeder in the Coastal Plain but more common in the Piedmont and Mountains.
Habitat: open, mixed and deciduous woodlands with a sparse understory, especially woodland openings and edges; rarely in open coniferous woodlands.

Similar Birds

Eastern Phoebe

Eastern Kingbird

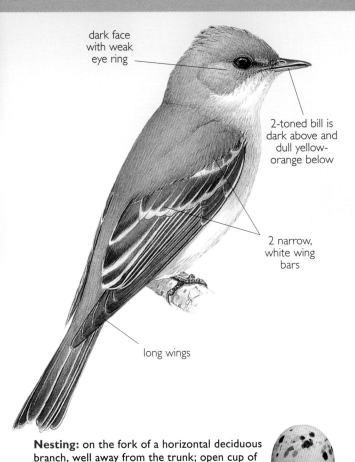

dark face with weak eye ring

2-toned bill is dark above and dull yellow-orange below

2 narrow, white wing bars

long wings

Nesting: on the fork of a horizontal deciduous branch, well away from the trunk; open cup of plants and lichen is bound with spider silk; whitish, darkly blotched eggs are 1 × ½ in; female incubates 3 eggs for 12–13 days.

Did You Know?

Sometimes you can hear the snap of a wood-pewee's bill closing around an insect.

Look For

Like other flycatchers, the Eastern Wood-Pewee loops out from exposed perches to snatch flying insects in midair, a technique often referred to as "flycatching" or "hawking."

Acadian Flycatcher
Empidonax virescens

The Acadian Flycatcher's quick, forceful *peet-sa* song is one of its key features, but learning to identify this bird is only half the fun. Its speedy, aerial courtship chases and the male's hovering flight displays are sights to behold—that is if you can survive the swarming hordes of bloodsucking mosquitoes deep within the swampy woodlands where this flycatcher is primarily found. • A standing dead tree or "planted" tree limb in your backyard may attract flycatchers that are looking for a hunting perch.

Other ID: large bill has dark upper mandible and pinkish yellow lower mandible; faint olive yellow breast; yellow belly and undertail coverts.
Size: L 5½–6 in; W 9 in.
Voice: song is a forceful *peet-sa;* call is a softer *peet;* may issue a loud, flickerlike *ti-ti-ti-ti-ti* during the breeding season.
Status: common breeder in the Coastal Plain; fairly common breeder in the Piedmont and Mountains.
Habitat: fairly mature deciduous woodlands, riparian woodlands and wooded swamps.

Similar Birds

Alder Flycatcher

Willow Flycatcher

Least Flycatcher

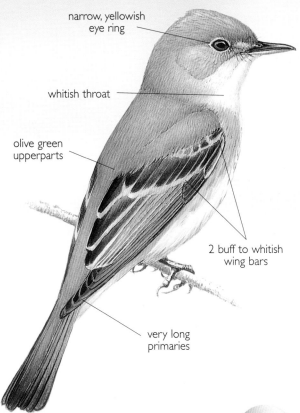

narrow, yellowish
eye ring

whitish throat

olive green
upperparts

2 buff to whitish
wing bars

very long
primaries

Nesting: low in a deciduous tree; female builds a loose cup nest from vegetation held together with spider silk; creamy white, lightly spotted eggs are ¾ × ½ in; female incubates 3 eggs for 13–15 days.

Did You Know?

Flycatchers are members of the family Tyrannidae, or "Tyrant Flycatchers," so-named because of their feisty, aggressive behavior.

Look For

The nest is built on a horizontal branch up to 20 feet above the ground and can be quite conspicuous because loose material often dangles from it.

Great Crested Flycatcher

Myiarchus crinitus

Loud, raucous calls give away the presence of the brightly colored Great Crested Flycatcher. This large flycatcher often inhabits forest edges and nests in woodlands throughout South Carolina. Unlike other eastern flycatchers, the Great Crested prefers to nest in a tree cavity or abandoned woodpecker hole, or sometimes uses a nest box intended for a bluebird. Once in a while, the Great Crested Flycatcher will decorate the nest entrance with a shed snakeskin or substitute translucent plastic wrap. The purpose of this practice is not fully understood, though it may make the nest less likely to be taken over by another bird or animal.

Other ID: dark olive brown upperparts; heavy black bill.
Size: *L* 8–9 in; *W* 13 in.
Voice: loud, whistled *wheep!* and a rolling *prrrrreet!*
Status: fairly common breeder.
Habitat: deciduous and mixed woodlands and forests, usually near openings or edges.

Similar Birds

Eastern Phoebe

Eastern Wood-Pewee
(p. 130)

Eastern Kingbird
(p. 136)

peaked, "crested" head

gray throat and upper breast

bright yellow belly and undertail coverts

reddish brown tail

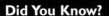

Nesting: in a tree cavity or nest box; nest is lined with soft material; heavily marked, creamy white to pale buff eggs are $7/8 \times 5/8$ in; female incubates 5 eggs for 13–15 days.

Did You Know?

Instead of cutting down large, dead trees, consider leaving a few standing. Many animals depend on tree cavities for shelter and nesting.

Look For

Follow the loud *wheep!* calls and watch for a show of bright yellow and rufous feathers to find this fly-catcher.

Eastern Kingbird
Tyrannus tyrannus

Sometimes referred to as the "Jekyll and Hyde" bird, the Eastern Kingbird is a gregarious fruit eater while wintering in South America and an antisocial, aggressive insect eater while nesting in North America. • The Eastern Kingbird fearlessly attacks crows, hawks and even humans that pass through its territory, pursuing and pecking at them until the threat has passed. No one familiar with the Eastern Kingbird's pugnacious behavior will refute its scientific name, *Tyrannus tyrannus*. This bird reveals a gentler side of its character in its quivering, butterfly-like courtship flight.

Other ID: black bill; no eye ring; white underparts; grayish breast; black legs; white-tipped tail.
Size: *L* 8½–9 in; *W* 15 in.
Voice: call is a quick, loud, chattering *kit-kit-kitter-ki-ter;* also a *buzzy dzee-dzee-dzee.*
Status: fairly common breeder; common migrant along the coast in fall.
Habitat: fields with scattered shrubs and trees or hedgerows, forest fringes, clearings, shrubby roadsides, towns and farmyards.

Similar Birds

Eastern Wood-Pewee
(p. 130)

Least Flycatcher

Eastern Phoebe

thin, orange-red crown
(rarely seen)

small head crest

dark gray to black
upperparts

Nesting: on a horizontal limb, stump or upturned tree root; cup nest is made of weeds, twigs and grass; darkly blotched, white to pinkish white eggs are 1 x ¾ in; female incubates 3–4 eggs for 14–18 days.

Did You Know?

Eastern Kingbirds are common and widespread. On a drive in the country you will likely spot at least one of these birds sitting on a fence or utility wire.

Look For

Eastern Kingbirds rarely walk or hop on the ground—they prefer to fly, even for very short distances.

Loggerhead Shrike
Lanius ludovicianus

This predatory songbird has very acute vision, and it often scans for small prey from a perch, then captures its prey in a fast, direct flight or a swooping dive. • Males display their hunting prowess by impaling prey on thorns or barbed wire. This behavior may also serve as a means of storing excess food during times of plenty. Shrikes seem to have an uncanny memory for the location of their food caches, and they have been known to find prey stored for up to eight months.

Other ID: *In flight:* white wing patches; white-edged tail.
Size: *L* 9 in; *W* 12 in.
Voice: high-pitched, hiccupy *bird-ee bird-ee* in summer; infrequently a harsh *shack-shack* year-round.
Status: species of special concern; local and declining; fairly common permanent resident in the Coastal Plain; uncommon in the lower Piedmont; rare elsewhere.
Habitat: grazed pastures and marginal and abandoned farmlands with hawthorn shrubs, fence posts, barbed wire and nearby wetlands.

Similar Birds

Northern Mockingbird
(p. 176)

Look For

Shrikes typically perch at the top of tall trees and on wires to survey the surrounding area for prey.

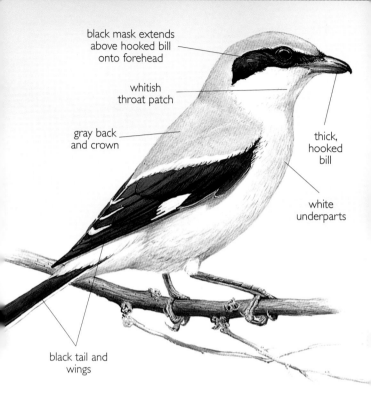

black mask extends
above hooked bill
onto forehead

whitish
throat patch

gray back
and crown

thick,
hooked
bill

white
underparts

black tail and
wings

Nesting: low in a shrub or small tree; the bulky
cup nest of twigs and grass is lined with animal
hair, feathers and plant down; pale eggs with dark
spots are 1 × ¾ in; female incubates 5–6 eggs
for 15–17 days.

Did You Know?

Unfortunately, habitat destruction and pesticide use have
caused serious declines in Loggerhead Shrike populations
across North America, from which the species has been slow
to recover. Also, many shrikes become traffic fatalities when
they fly low across roads to prey on insects attracted to the
warm pavement.

White-eyed Vireo
Vireo griseus

This species is renowned for its complex vocalizations—a single White-eyed Vireo can have a repertoire of a dozen or more songs. This vireo is also an excellent vocal mimic and may incorporate the calls of other bird species in its own songs! • Even more cryptic than the bird itself is the location of its precious nest. Intricately woven from grass, twigs, bark, lichen, moss, plant down, leaves and the fibrous paper from a wasp nest, the nest of the White-eyed Vireo is hung between the forking branches of a tree or shrub.

Other ID: olive gray upperparts; white underparts; 2 whitish wing bars; dark wings and tail.
Size: *L* 5 in; *W* 7½ in.
Voice: loud, snappy, 3–9-note song: *quick, bring-the-beer check!*
Status: common breeder and migrant; occasionally winters in the lower Coastal Plain.
Habitat: dense, shrubby undergrowth and thickets in open, swampy, deciduous woodlands, overgrown fields, young second-growth woodlands, woodland clearings and along woodlot edges.

Similar Birds

Red-eyed Vireo
(p. 142)

Pine Warbler
(p. 190)

Yellow-throated Vireo

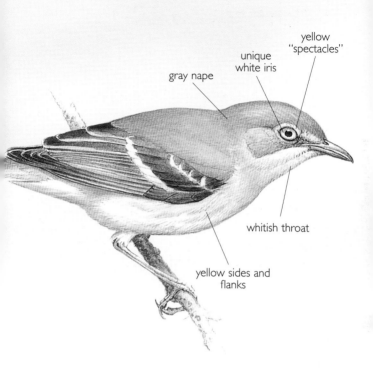

gray nape

unique
white iris

yellow
"spectacles"

whitish throat

yellow sides and
flanks

Nesting: in a deciduous shrub or small tree; cup nest hangs from a horizontal fork; lightly speckled, white eggs are ¾ × ⁹⁄₁₆ in; pair incubates 4 eggs for 13–15 days; both adults feed the young.

Did You Know?

When insects are scarce, White-eyed Vireos will eat berries, preferably green briar or honeysuckle. The tangled thickets also provide shelter.

Look For

The color of the bird's iris can help determine age: a juvenile White-eyed Vireo has dark eyes that change to a unique white color as the bird matures.

Red-eyed Vireo
Vireo olivaceus

Capable of delivering about 40 phrases per minute, the male Red-eyed Vireo can out-sing any one of his courting neighbors. One tenacious male set a record by singing 21,000 phrases in one day! Although you may still hear the Red-eyed Vireo singing five or six hours after other songbirds have ceased for the day, this bird is not easy to spot. It is usually concealed in its olive brown plumage among the foliage of deciduous trees. Its red eyes, unusual among songbirds, are even trickier to spot without a good pair of binoculars.

Other ID: black-bordered, olive cheek; olive green upperparts; white to pale gray underparts.
Size: *L* 6 in; *W* 10 in.
Voice: call is a short, scolding *rreeah*; song is a series of quick, continuous, variable phrases with pauses in between: *look-up, way-up, tree-top, see-me, here-I-am!*
Status: common breeder and migrant.
Habitat: deciduous or mixed woodlands with a shrubby understory.

Similar Birds

White-eyed Vireo
(p. 140)

Tennessee Warbler

white eyebrow

blue-gray crown

dark eye line

red eyes

Nesting: in a tree or shrub; hanging cup nest is made of grass, roots, spider silk and cocoons; darkly spotted, white eggs are ¾ × ½ in; female incubates 4 eggs for 11–14 days.

Did You Know?

If a Brown-headed Cow-bird parasitizes its nest, a Red-eyed Vireo will respond by abandoning the nest or by raising the cow-bird young with its own.

Look For

The Red-eyed Vireo perches with a hunched stance and hops with its body turned diagonally to its direction of travel.

Blue Jay

Cyanocitta cristata

The Blue Jay is the only member of the corvid family dressed in blue in South Carolina. White-flecked wing feathers and sharply defined facial features make this bird easy to recognize. • Jays can be quite aggressive when competing for sunflower seeds and peanuts at backyard feeding stations, and rarely hesitate to drive away smaller birds, squirrels or even threatening cats. Even the Great Horned Owl is not too formidable a predator for a group of these brave, boisterous mobsters to harass.

Other ID: blue upperparts; white underparts; black bill.

Size: L 11–12 in; W 16 in.

Voice: noisy, screaming *jay-jay-jay;* nasal *queedle queedle queedle-queedle* sounds like a muted trumpet; often imitates various sounds, including calls of other birds.

Status: common permanent resident; more numerous in fall as migrants pass through.

Habitat: mixed deciduous forests, agricultural areas, scrubby fields and townsites.

Similar Birds

Belted Kingfisher
(p. 120)

Eastern Bluebird
(p. 168)

blue crest

black "necklace"

dark bars and white flecking on wings

dark bars and white corners on blue tail

Nesting: in a tree or tall shrub; pair builds a bulky stick nest; greenish, buff or pale eggs, spotted with gray and brown, are 1⅛ × ¾ in; pair incubates 4–5 eggs for 16–18 days.

Did You Know?

Blue Jays store food from feeders in trees and other places for later use.

Look For

When you hear the call of a Red-shouldered Hawk, American Crow or even a neighborhood cat, make sure it is not really a Blue Jay imitating their calls.

American Crow

Corvus brachyrhynchos

The noise that most often emanates from this treetop squawker seems unrepresentative of its intelligence. However, this wary, clever bird is also an impressive mimic, able to whine like a dog and laugh or cry like a human. • American Crows have flourished in spite of considerable efforts, over many generations, to reduce their numbers. As ecological generalists, crows can survive in a wide variety of habitats and conditions. In January, when crows in South Carolina are busy capturing frogs and lizards in thriving wetlands, crows in more northerly locales are searching snow-covered fields for mice or carrion.

Other ID: glossy, purple-black plumage; black bill and legs; short, square-shaped tail.
Size: *L* 17–21-in; *W* 3 ft.
Voice: distinctive, far-carrying, repetitive *caw-caw-caw*.
Status: common permanent resident.
Habitat: urban areas, agricultural fields and other open areas with scattered woodlands.

Similar Birds

Fish Crow

Common Raven

Common Grackle

slim, sleek head
and throat

Nesting: in a tree or on a utility pole; large stick-and-branch nest is lined with fur and soft plant materials; darkly blotched, gray-green to blue-green eggs are 1⅝ × 1⅛ in; female incubates 4–6 eggs for about 18 days.

Did You Know?

Crows are family oriented, and the young from the previous year may help their parents to raise the nestlings.

Look For

Crows will often drop walnuts or clams from great heights onto a hard surface to crack the shells, one of the few examples of birds using objects to manipulate food.

Purple Martin
Progne subis

These large swallows will entertain you throughout spring and summer if you set up luxurious "condo complexes" for them. You can watch martin adults spiral around their accommodations in pursuit of flying insects, while their young perch clumsily at the cavity openings. Purple Martins once nested in natural tree hollows and in cliff crevices but now have virtually abandoned these in favor of human-made housing. • To avoid the invasion of aggressive House Sparrows or European Starlings, it is essential for martin condos to be cleaned out and closed up after each nesting season.

Other ID: pointed wings; small bill. *Female:* sooty gray underparts.
Size: *L* 7–8 in; *W* 18 in.
Voice: rich, fluty, robinlike *pew-pew*, often heard in flight.
Status: common breeder and migrant except at the highest elevations in the Mountains.
Habitat: semi-open areas, often near water.

Similar Birds

European Starling
(p. 180)

Barn Swallow
(p. 150)

Northern Rough-
winged Swallow

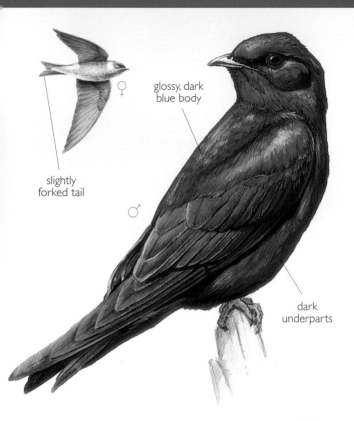

glossy, dark blue body

slightly forked tail

♀

♂

dark underparts

Nesting: communal; in a human-made bird-house or hollowed-out gourd; nest is made of feathers, grass and mud; white eggs are 1 × ⅝ in; female incubates 4–5 eggs for 15–18 days.

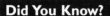

Did You Know?

The Purple Martin is North America's largest swallow.

Look For

Purple Martins are more often attracted to martin condo complexes erected in open areas, high on a pole and near a body of water.

Barn Swallow
Hirundo rustica

When you encounter this bird, you might first
notice its distinctive, deeply forked tail—or you
might just find yourself repeatedly ducking to
avoid the dives of a protective parent. Barn
Swallows once nested on cliffs, but they are now
found more frequently nesting on barns, boat-
houses and under bridges and house eaves. The
messiness of the young and aggressiveness of the
parents often motivate people to remove nests just
as nesting season is beginning. But this bird's close
association with humans allows us to observe the
normally secretive reproductive cycle of birds.

Other ID: blue-black upperparts; long,
pointed wings.
Size: *L* 7 in; *W* 15 in.
Voice: continuous, twittering
chatter: *zip-zip-zip* or *kvick-
kvick.*
Status: common breeder and
migrant; uncommon in winter at
the coast.
Habitat: open rural and urban areas
where bridges, culverts and buildings are
found near water.

Similar Birds

Cliff Swallow

Purple Martin
(p. 148)

rufous forehead
and throat

black "necklace"

rust- to buff-
colored
underparts

long, deeply
forked tail

Nesting: singly or in small, loose colonies; on a human-made structure under an overhang; half or full cup nest is made of mud, grass and straw; brown-spotted, white eggs are ¾ × ½ in; pair incubates 4–7 eggs for 13–17 days.

Did You Know?

The Barn Swallow is a natural pest controller, feeding on insects that are often harmful to crops and livestock.

Look For

Barn Swallows roll mud into small balls and build their nests one mouthful of mud at a time.

Carolina Chickadee
Poecile carolinensis

Fidgety, friendly Carolina Chickadees are familiar to anyone with a backyard feeder well stocked with sunflower seeds and peanut butter. These agile birds even hang upside down to pluck berries and snatch insects. Like some woodpeckers and nut-hatches, the Carolina Chickadee will hoard food for later in the season when food may become scarce. • It's hard to imagine a chickadee using its tiny bill to excavate a nesting cavity, but come breeding season, this energetic little bird can be found hammering out a hollow in a rotting tree.

Other ID: grayish nape; white underparts and buffy flanks.
Size: *L* 4¾ in; *W* 7½ in.
Voice: whistling song has 4 clear notes sounding like *fee-bee fee-bay.*
Status: common permanent resident.
Habitat: deciduous and mixed woods, riparian woodlands, groves and isolated shade trees; frequents urban areas.

Similar Birds

Red-breasted Nuthatch   Blackpoll Warbler

black cap and "bib"

white cheek

gray upperparts and secondaries

Nesting: excavates or enlarges a tree cavity; may also use a nest box; cavity is lined with soft material; white eggs, marked with reddish brown are ½ × ⅜ in; female incubates 5–8 eggs for 11–14 days.

Did You Know?

Chickadee flocks are often made up of close family members that vigorously defend the same territory for many generations.

Look For

Alert Carolina Chickadees are often the first to issue alarm calls, warning other birds that danger is near.

Tufted Titmouse

Baeolophus bicolor

This bird's amusing feeding antics and insatiable appetite keep curious observers entertained at bird feeders. Grasping a sunflower seed with its tiny feet, the dexterous Tufted Titmouse will strike its dainty bill repeatedly against the hard outer coating to expose the inner core. • A breeding pair of Tufted Titmice will maintain their bond throughout the year, even when joining small, mixed flocks for the cold winter months. The titmouse family bond is so strong that the young from one breeding season will occasionally stay with their parents long enough to help with nesting and feeding duties the following year.

Other ID: gray upperparts; white underparts; pale face.
Size: L 6–6½ in; W 10 in.
Voice: noisy, scolding call, like that of a chickadee; song is a whistled *peter peter* or *peter peter peter*.
Status: common permanent resident.
Habitat: deciduous woodlands, groves and suburban parks with large, mature trees.

Look For

Easily identified by its gray crest and upperparts and black forehead, the tufted titmouse can often be seen at feeders. Titmice always choose the largest sunflower seeds available to them at feeders, and during winter, they often cache food in bark crevices.

gray crest

black forehead

buffy flanks

Nesting: in a natural cavity or woodpecker nest lined with soft vegetation, moss and animal hair; heavily spotted, white eggs are ⅝ × ½ in; female incubates 5–6 eggs for 12–14 days.

Did You Know?

Nesting pairs search for soft nest-lining material in late winter, and you may be able to attract them with an offering of the hair that has accumulated in your hairbrush.

White-breasted Nuthatch

Sitta carolinensis

Its upside-down antics and noisy, nasal call make the White-breasted Nuthatch a favorite among novice birders. Whether you spot this black-capped bullet spiraling headfirst down a tree or clinging to the underside of a branch in search of invertebrates, the nuthatch's odd behavior deserves a second glance. • Comparing the White-breasted Nuthatch to the Carolina Chickadee, both regular visitors to backyard feeders, is a perfect starting point for introductory birding. While both have dark crowns and gray backs, the nuthatch's foraging behavior and undulating flight pattern are distinctive.

Other ID: white underparts; white face; straight bill; short legs. *Female:* dark gray cap.
Size: *L* 5½–6 in; *W* 11 in.
Voice: song is a fast, nasal *yank-hank yank-hank;* calls include *ha-ha-ha ha-ha-ha, ank ank* and *ip.*
Status: common permanent resident.
Habitat: mixed forests, woodlots and backyards.

Similar Birds

Red-breasted Nuthatch

Carolina Chickadee
(p. 152)

Brown-headed Nuthatch (p. 158)

rusty undertail
coverts

short tail

gray-blue
back

dark crown

♀

♂

Nesting: in a natural cavity or an abandoned
woodpecker nest; female lines the cavity with soft
material; white eggs, speckled with brown are
¾ × ½ in; female incubates 5–8 eggs for 12–14 days.

Did You Know?

The scientific name
carolinensis means "of
Carolina"—the first
White-breasted Nuthatch
specimen was collected in
South Carolina.

Look For

Nuthatches grasp the tree
through foot power alone,
unlike woodpeckers, which
use their tails to brace
themselves against tree
trunks.

Brown-headed Nuthatch
Sitta pusilla

Brown-headed Nuthatches are endemic to the pine forests of the Deep South, making them one of the very few bird species found exclusively in the United States. They are common throughout South Carolina, except in the Mountains, where they are rare. • The Brown-headed Nuthatch is one of very few North American birds to use tools. It holds a loose piece of pine bark in its bill and uses it to pry off other bark flakes, uncovering hidden insects. The tool may be carried from tree to tree or discarded once prey is found.

Other ID: dull blue-gray back and wings; whitish underparts; short tail.
Size: L 4½ in; W 7½ in.
Voice: squeaky 2-noted "rubber ducky" calls.
Status: common permanent resident in the Coastal Plain; fairly common permanent resident in the Piedmont; rare at lower elevations in the Mountains.
Habitat: open and mixed pine woodlands.

Similar Birds

Red-breasted Nuthatch

White-breasted Nuthatch (p. 156)

Brown Creeper

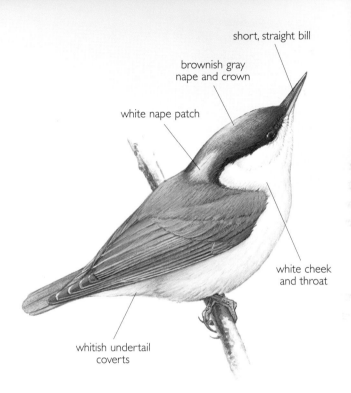

short, straight bill

brownish gray
nape and crown

white nape patch

white cheek
and throat

whitish undertail
coverts

Nesting: pair excavates a nest cavity in a pine
snag or fence post; cavity is lined with wood
chips and grass; profusely speckled, white eggs
are ⅝ × ½ in; male feeds female as she incubates
4–7 eggs for 13–15 days.

Did You Know?

A young male helper may
join the breeding pair to
assist with excavating the
nest cavity, gathering the
soft nest lining or feeding
the nestlings.

Look For

In winter, this bird is often
found in larger, multispecies
flocks that include Eastern
Bluebirds, Carolina Chickadees, Tufted Titmice and
Pine Warblers.

Carolina Wren
Thryothorus ludovicianus

The energetic and cheerful Carolina Wren can
be shy and retiring, often hiding deep inside
dense shrubbery. The best opportunity for viewing
this particularly vocal wren is when it sits on a
conspicuous perch while unleashing its impressive
song. Pairs perform lively "duets" at any time of
day and in any season. The duet often begins with
introductory chatter by the female, followed by
innumerable ringing variations of *tea-kettle tea-
kettle tea-kettle tea* from her mate. • Carolina
Wrens readily nest in the brushy thickets of an
overgrown backyard or in an obscure nook or
crevice in a house or barn. If conditions are favor-
able, two broods may be raised in a single season.

Other ID: rusty cheek; white throat; longish,
slightly downcurved bill; tail is
rather long for a wren.
Size: L 5½ in; W 7½ in.
Voice: loud, repetitious *tea-kettle
tea-kettle tea-kettle tea;* female often
chatters while the male sings.
Status: common permanent resident.
Habitat: dense forest undergrowth,
especially shrubby tangles and thickets.

Similar Birds

House Wren

Winter Wren

rich brown upperparts
including nape and crown

bold white
eyebrow

rich buff-colored
underparts

Nesting: in a nest box or natural or artificial cavity; nest is lined with soft materials, including snakeskin at the entrance; brown-blotched, white eggs are ¾ × ⅝ in; female incubates 4–5 eggs for 12–16 days.

Did You Know?

In mild winters, Carolina Wren populations remain stable, but frigid temperatures can temporarily decimate an otherwise healthy population.

Look For

A nesting Carolina Wren will not hesitate to give intruders a severe scolding but remains hidden all the while.

Marsh Wren
Cistothorus palustris

Fueled by newly emerged aquatic insects, the Marsh Wren zips about in short bursts through the tall grass and cattails that surround our coastal wetlands. This expert hunter catches flying insects with lightning speed, but don't expect to see the Marsh Wren in action—it is a reclusive bird that prefers to remain hidden deep within its dense marshland habitat. This bird's distinctive song, reminiscent of an old-fashioned treadle sewing machine, is more likely to inform you of its presence.

Other ID: long, thin, downcurved bill; white to light brown upperparts; rufous sides.
Size: *L* 5 in; *W* 6 in.
Voice: rapid, rattling, staccato warble sounds; call is a harsh *chek*.
Status: fairly common permanent resident in coastal areas; fairly common migrant statewide; each year a few birds winter in the upper Coastal Plain.
Habitat: freshwater, saltwater and brackish wetlands surrounded by tall grass, bulrushes or cattails interspersed with open water; occasionally in tall grass–sedge marshes.

Similar Birds

Sedge Wren   House Wren

Carolina Wren
(p. 160)

dark crown

bold, white eyebrow

black triangle on upper back is streaked with white

white chin and belly

Nesting: in a brackish or salt marsh among cattails or tall emergent vegetation; globelike nest is woven from cattails, bulrushes, weeds and grass and lined with cattail down; darkly marked, white to pale brown eggs are ⅝ × ½ in; female incubates 4–6 eggs for 12–16 days.

Did You Know?

The scientific name *palustris* is Latin for "marsh." This bird was formerly known as "Long-billed Marsh Wren."

Look For

The Worthington's Marsh Wren is a subspecies that breeds near the coast. It is considerably grayer than the migrants that travel through the state.

Ruby-crowned Kinglet

Regulus calendula

While in South Carolina, Ruby-crowned Kinglets flit among the branches along with a colorful assortment of warblers and vireos. This bird might be mistaken for an *Empidonax* flycatcher, but the kinglet's frequent hovering and energetic wing-flicking behavior set it apart from look-alikes. The wing flicking is thought to startle insects into movement, allowing the kinglet to spot them and pounce. • Look for this bird at any location in the state in winter—it is abundant and widespread.

Other ID: olive green upperparts; dark wings; whitish to yellowish underparts; flicks its wings.
Size: *L* 4 in; *W* 7½ in.
Voice: song is an accelerating and rising *tea-tea-tea-tew-tew-tew look-at-Me, look-at-Me, look-at-Me; digit, digit* call.
Status: common to abundant winter resident.
Habitat: mixed woodlands and pure coniferous forests, often near wet forest openings and edges.

Similar Birds

Golden-crowned Kinglet

Orange-crowned Warbler

Yellow-bellied Flycatcher

bold, broken
eye ring

male's small,
red crown is
usually hidden

short, dark tail

2 white wing bars

♀

♂

Nesting: does not nest in South
Carolina; nests mainly in Canada and
the western U.S.; usually in a conifer;
female builds hanging nest of lichen,
twigs and leaves; brown-spotted, white
to pale buff eggs are ½ × ⅜ in; female incubates 7–8 eggs for 13–14 days.

Did You Know?

A female can lay an
impressively large clutch
with up to 12 eggs, which
together often weigh as
much as she does!

Look For

Both sexes call their distinct
digit, digit calls to each other
as they forage with other
species in the winter mixed
flocks of chickadees, titmice
and nuthatches.

Blue-gray Gnatcatcher
Polioptila caerulea

The fidgety Blue-gray Gnatcatcher is constantly on the move. It holds its tail upward like a wren and issues a quiet, banjolike twang while flitting restlessly from shrub to shrub. • Gnatcatcher pairs remain close once a bond is established, and both parents share the responsibilities of nest building, incubation and raising the young. When young gnatcatchers are ready to fly, they leave the nest for the cover of dense shrubby tangles along woodland edges, where they feed on gnats and many other insects.

Other ID: no wing bars; long tail; black uppertail.
Nonbreeding: pale gray underparts.
Size: L 4½ in; W 6 in.
Voice: song is a faint, airy *puree;* call is a banjolike, high-pitched *twang.*
Status: common to fairly common breeder; fairly common in the Coastal Plain in winter.
Habitat: deciduous woodlands along streams, ponds, lakes and swamps; also in orchards, along woodland edges and oak savannas.

Similar Birds

Golden-crowned Kinglet   Ruby-crowned Kinglet
(p. 164)

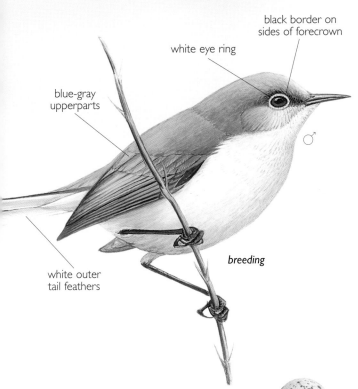

black border on sides of forecrown

white eye ring

blue-gray upperparts

♂

breeding

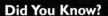

white outer tail feathers

Nesting: cup nest is made of plant fibers, bark chips and is decorated with lichens; nest is lined with soft hair and plants; pale bluish white, dotted eggs are ⅝ × ½ in; female incubates 3–5 eggs for 11–15 days.

Did You Know?

The scientific name *Polioptila* means "gray feather," while *caerulea* means "blue."

Look For

Foraging gnatcatchers often flash their white outer tail feathers, an action that reflects light and may scare insects into flight.

Eastern Bluebird
Sialia sialis

The Eastern Bluebird's enticing colors are like those of a warm setting sun against a deep blue sky. • This cavity nester's survival has been put to the test—populations have declined in the presence of the competitive, introduced House Sparrow and European Starling. The removal of standing dead trees has also diminished nest site availability. Thankfully, bluebird enthusiasts and organizations developed "bluebird trails" and mounted nest boxes on fence posts along highways and rural roads, allowing Eastern Bluebird numbers to gradually recover.

Other ID: dark bill; dark legs. *Female:* thin, white eye ring; gray-brown head and back are tinged with blue; blue wings and tail; paler chestnut underparts.
Size: *L* 7 in; *W* 13 in.
Voice: song is a rich, warbling *turr, turr-lee, turr-lee;* call is a chittering *pew.*
Status: common permanent resident.
Habitat: cropland fencelines, meadows, fallow and abandoned fields, pastures, forest clearings and edges, golf courses, large lawns and cemeteries.

Similar Birds

Indigo Bunting
(p. 210)

Look For

The Eastern Bluebird uses an elevated perch as a base from which to hunt insects. It also feeds on berries and is especially attracted to wild grapes, sumac and currants.

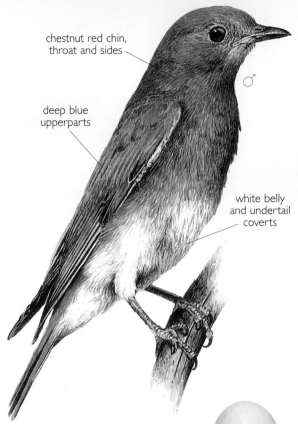

chestnut red chin, throat and sides

deep blue upperparts

♂

white belly and undertail coverts

Nesting: in a natural cavity or nest box; female builds a cup nest of grass, weed stems and small twigs; pale blue eggs are ⅞ × ⅝ in; female incubates 4–5 eggs for 13–16 days.

Did You Know?

Usually it is difficult to tell the sex of juvenile birds, but with bluebirds there are visible differences. Juvenule of both sexes are gray-brown with pale streaking above and dark spotting below, but males have blue-tinged wings and tail.

Wood Thrush
Hylocichla mustelina

The loud, warbled notes of the Wood Thrush once resounded through our woodlands, but forest fragmentation and urban sprawl have eliminated much of this bird's nesting habitat. These changes have allowed the invasion of common, open-area predators and parasites, such as raccoons, skunks, crows, jays and cowbirds. Traditionally, these predators had little access to nests that were hidden deep within vast hardwood forests. Many forests that have been urbanized or developed for agriculture now host families of American Robins rather than the once-prominent Wood Thrushes.

Other ID: plump body; streaked cheeks; brown wings, rump and tail.
Size: L 8 in; W 13 in.
Voice: *Male:* bell-like phrases of 3–5 notes, with each note at a different pitch and followed by a trill: *Will you live with me? Way up high in a tree, I'll come right down and…seeee!*
Status: fairly common breeder and migrant.
Habitat: moist, mature and preferably undisturbed deciduous woodlands and mixed forests.

Similar Birds

Swainson's Thrush   Hermit Thrush

bold white
eye ring

rusty head
and back

large, black
spots on white
breast, sides
and flanks

Nesting: low in a fork of a deciduous tree; female builds a bulky cup nest of vegetation, held together with mud and lined with softer materials; eggs are 1 × ¾ in; female incubates 3–4 pale, greenish blue eggs for 13–14 days.

Did You Know?

Henry David Thoreau considered the Wood Thrush's song to be the most beautiful of avian sounds. The male can even sing two notes at once!

Look For

Wood Thrushes forage on the ground or glean vegetation for insects and other invertebrates.

American Robin
Turdus migratorius

Come March, the familiar song of the American Robin may wake you early if you are a light sleeper. This abundant bird adapts easily to urban areas and often works from dawn until after dusk when there is a nest to be built or hungry, young mouths to feed. • The robin's bright orange belly contrasts with its dark head and wings, making this bird easy to identify. • In winter, fruit trees may attract flocks of robins, which gather to eat the fruit once insects and earthworms become harder to find.

Other ID: incomplete, white eye ring; gray-brown back; white undertail coverts.
Size: *L* 10 in; *W* 17 in.
Voice: song is an evenly spaced warble: *cheerily-cheer-up cheerio.*
Status: common breeder in the Piedmont and Mountains, less common at the coast; abundant migrant and winter resident, especially in the Coastal Plain.
Habitat: *Breeding:* residential lawns and gardens, pastures, urban parks, broken forests, bogs and river shorelines. *Winter:* near fruit-bearing trees and springs.

Similar Birds

Orchard Oriole
(p. 222)

Look For

A hunting robin with its head tilted to the side isn't listening for prey—it is actually looking for movements in the soil.

black head

black-tipped, yellow bill

dark gray head

♂

♀

white throat is streaked with black

brick red breast is darker on male

Nesting: in a tree or shrub; cup nest is built of grass, moss, bark and mud; light blue eggs are 1⅛ × ¾ in; female incubates 4 eggs for 11–16 days; raises up to 3 broods per year.

Did You Know?

American Robins do not use nest boxes; they prefer platforms for their nests. They usually raise two broods per year, and the male cares for the fledglings from the first brood while the female incubates the second clutch of eggs.

Gray Catbird

Dumetella carolinensis

The Gray Catbird is an accomplished mimic that may fool you as it shuffles through underbrush and dense riparian shrubs, calling its catlike meow. Its mimicking talents are further enhanced by its ability to sing two notes at once, using each side of its syrinx individually. • The Gray Catbird vigilantly defends its territory against sparrows, robins, cowbirds and other intruders. It destroys the eggs and nestlings of other songbirds and takes on an intense defensive posture if approached, screaming and even attempting to hit an intruder.

Other ID: dark gray overall; black eyes, bill and legs.
Size: L 8½–9 in; W 11 in.
Voice: calls include a catlike *meoww* and a harsh *check-check;* song is a variety of warbles, squeaks and mimicked phrases interspersed with a *mew* call.
Status: common breeder; common winter resident in the Coastal Plain; abundant migrant statewide.
Habitat: dense thickets, brambles, shrubby or brushy areas and hedgerows, often near water.

Similar Birds

Northern Mockingbird
(p. 176)

Look For

If you catch a glimpse of this bird during breeding season, watch the male raise his long, slender tail into the air to show off his rust-colored undertail coverts.

long tail is dark gray to black

black cap

chestnut under-tail coverts

Nesting: in a dense shrub or thicket; bulky cup nest is made of twigs, leaves and grass; greenish blue eggs are ⅞ × ⅝ in; female incubates 4 eggs for 12–15 days.

Did You Know?

Gray Catbirds vigorously defend their nesting territories, often to the benefit of neighboring wood-warblers, towhees and sparrows. They are among the few birds able to recognize cowbird eggs, which female catbirds readily eject from the nest.

Northern Mockingbird

Mimus polyglottos

The Northern Mockingbird has an amazing vocal repertoire that includes over 400 different song types, which it belts out incessantly throughout the breeding season, serenading into the night during a full moon. Mockingbirds can imitate almost anything. In some instances, they replicate notes so accurately that even computerized sound analysis is unable to detect the difference between the original source and the mockingbird's imitation.

Other ID: gray upperparts; 2 thin, white wing bars; light gray underparts. *Juvenile:* paler overall; spotted breast. *In flight:* large white patch at base of black primaries.
Size: *L* 10 in; *W* 14 in.
Voice: song is a medley of mimicked phrases, with the phrases often repeated 3 times or more; calls include a harsh *chair* and *chewk*.
Status: common permanent resident; less common in the Mountains.
Habitat: hedges, suburban gardens and orchard margins with an abundance of available fruit; hedgerows of multiflora roses are especially important in winter.

Similar Birds

Loggerhead Shrike
(p. 138)

Gray Catbird
(p. 174)

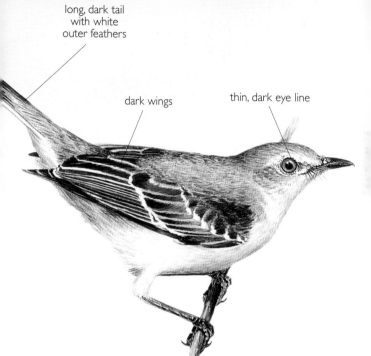

long, dark tail with white outer feathers

dark wings

thin, dark eye line

Nesting: often in a small shrub or small tree; cup nest is built with twigs and plants; brown-blotched, bluish gray to greenish eggs are 1 × ⅝ in; female incubates 3–4 eggs for 12–13 days.

Did You Know?

The scientific name *polyglottos* is Greek for "many tongues" and refers to this bird's ability to mimic a wide variety of sounds.

Look For

The Northern Mockingbird's energetic territorial dance is delightful to watch, as males square off in what appears to be a swordless fencing duel.

Brown Thrasher
Toxostoma rufum

The Brown Thrasher shares the streaked breast of a thrush and the long tail of a catbird, but it has a temper all its own. Because it nests close to the ground, the Brown Thrasher defends its nest with a vengeance, attacking snakes and other nest robbers sometimes to the point of drawing blood. • Biologists have estimated that the male Brown Thrasher is capable of producing up to 3000 distinctive song phrases—the most extensive vocal repertoire of any North American bird.

Other ID: reddish brown upperparts and long, rufous tail; orange-yellow eyes.
Size: L 11½ in; W 13 in.
Voice: sings a large variety of phrases, with each phrase usually repeated twice: *dig-it dig-it, hoe-it hoe-it, pull-it-up pull-it-up.*
Status: common permanent resident; less common in the Mountains in winter.
Habitat: dense shrubs and thickets, overgrown pastures, woodland edges and brushy areas, rarely close to urban areas.

Similar Birds

Wood Thrush
(p. 170)

Veery

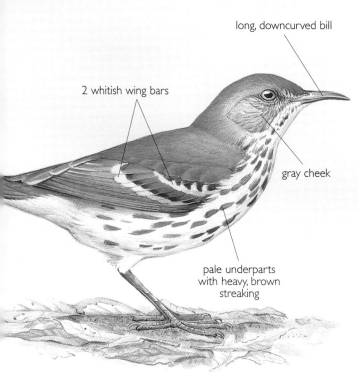

long, downcurved bill

2 whitish wing bars

gray cheek

pale underparts
with heavy, brown
streaking

Nesting: usually in a low shrub; often on the
ground; cup nest made of grass, twigs and leaves
is lined with vegetation; pale blue eggs, dotted
with reddish brown are 1 × ¾ in; pair incubates
4 eggs for 11–14 days.

Did You Know?

Fencing shrubby, wooded
areas bordering wetlands
and streams can prevent
cattle from devastating
thrasher nesting habitat.

Look For

You might catch only a flash
of rufous as the Brown
Thrasher flies from one
thicket to another in its
shrubby understory habitat.

European Starling
Sturnus vulgaris

The European Starling did not hesitate to make itself known across North America after being released in New York's Central Park in 1890 and 1891. This highly adaptable bird not only took over the nest sites of native cavity nesters, such as Tree Swallows and Red-headed Woodpeckers, but it also learned to mimic the sounds of Killdeers, Red-tailed Hawks, Soras and meadowlarks. • Look for European Starlings in massive evening roosts under bridges or on buildings in late summer and through the winter months.

Other ID: dark eyes; short, squared tail.
Nonbreeding: feather tips are heavily spotted with white and buff.
Size: *L* 8½ in; *W* 16 in.
Voice: variety of whistles, squeaks and gurgles; imitates other birds.
Status: common to abundant permanent resident.
Habitat: *Breeding:* cities, towns, residential areas, farmyards, woodland fringes and clearings. *Winter:* near feedlots and pastures.

Similar Birds

Rusty Blackbird

Brown-headed Cowbird (p. 220)

iridescent, purple-black
head, neck and breast

yellow bill

glossy, green back
with buffy spots

greenish black
underparts

breeding

Nesting: in an abandoned woodpecker cavity,
natural cavity or nest box; nest is made of grass,
twigs and straw; bluish to greenish white eggs
are 1⅛ × ⅞ in; female incubates 4–6 eggs for
12–14 days.

Did You Know?

Starlings were brought to
New York as part of the
local Shakespeare society's
plan to introduce all the
birds mentioned in their
favorite author's writings.

Look For

It can be confused with
a blackbird, but note the
European Starling's shorter
tail and bright yellow bill.

Cedar Waxwing
Bombycilla cedrorum

Flocks of handsome Cedar Waxwings gorge on berries during late winter and spring. Waxwings have a remarkable ability to digest a wide variety of berries, some of which are inedible or even poisonous to humans. If the fruits have fermented, these birds will show definite signs of tipsiness.
• Practiced observers learn to recognize these birds by their high-pitched, trilling calls. Flocks are highly nomadic, and numbers vary each year.

Other ID: brown upperparts; yellow wash on belly; gray rump; white undertail coverts.
Size: *L* 7 in; *W* 12 in.
Voice: faint, high-pitched, trilled whistle: *tseee-tseee-tseee.*
Status: common winter resident; uncommon breeder in the Mountains and probably upper Piedmont; may be expanding its breeding range farther into the lower Piedmont.
Habitat: wooded residential parks and gardens, overgrown fields, forest edges, second-growth, riparian and open woodlands; often near fruit trees and water.

Similar Birds

Northern Cardinal
(p. 208), female

Look For

If a bird's crop is full, it will continue to pluck fruit and pass it down the line like a bucket brigade, until the fruit is gulped down by a still-hungry bird.

cinnamon crest

black mask

small red "drops" on wings

yellow terminal tail band

Nesting: in a tree or shrub; cup nest is made of twigs, moss and lichen; darkly spotted, bluish to gray eggs are $7/8 \times 5/8$ in; female incubates 3–5 eggs for 12–16 days.

Did You Know?

The yellow tail band and red wing tips of the Cedar Waxwing get their color from pigments in the berries that these birds eat. Planting native berry-producing trees and shrubs in your backyard can attract Cedar Waxwings and will often encourage them to nest in your area. Holly and viburnum berries are favorites of waxwings in our region.

Northern Parula

Parula americana

Northern Parulas are common residents of habitats that contain an abundance of Spanish moss, in which the birds nest. They are also common in conifer-dominated mountain stream corridors. The young spend the first few weeks of their lives enclosed in a fragile, sock-like nest suspended from a tree branch. • Parula has two correct pronunciations: *PAIR-yuh-luh* or *PAIR-uh-luh;* the pronunciation *puh-ROO-luh,* although popular, is incorrect.

Other ID: 2 bold white wing bars; white belly and flanks.
Size: *L* 4½ in; *W* 7 in.
Voice: song is a rising buzzy trill ending with an abrupt lower *zip*.
Status: common breeder in the Coastal Plain and Mountains and fairly common in the Piedmont; rare in winter in the Coastal Plain.
Habitat: *Breeding:* moist coniferous forests, humid riparian or swampy deciduous woodlands, especially with hanging lichens. *In migration:* woodlands or areas with tall shrubs.

Similar Birds

Cerulean Warbler   Blue-winged Warbler   Yellow-rumped Warbler
(p. 186)

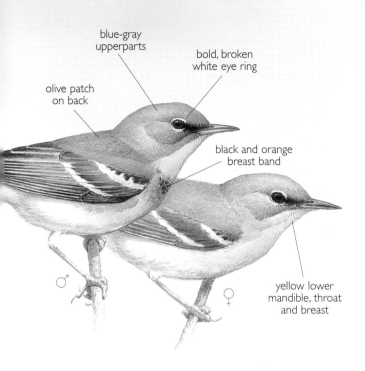

blue-gray
upperparts

bold, broken
white eye ring

olive patch
on back

black and orange
breast band

♂

♀

yellow lower
mandible, throat
and breast

Nesting: usually in a conifer; small hanging nest is woven by the female into hanging strands of tree lichens; may add lichens to a dense cluster of conifer boughs; brown-marked, whitish eggs are ⅝ × ½ in; pair incubates 4–5 eggs for 12–14 days.

Did You Know?

In spring, Northern Parulas are among the earliest warblers to return to breed in South Carolina.

Look For

Because we often see warblers from below, the Parula's bold chest, with yellow that extends all the way to the tip of the lower bill, is distinctive.

Yellow-rumped Warbler

Dendroica coronata

The Yellow-rumped Warbler is the most abundant and widespread wood-warbler in North America. This species comes in two forms: the common, white-throated "Myrtle Warbler" of the East (found in our state), and the yellow-throated "Audubon's Warbler" of the West (very rare in our state).

• This bird can be found easily in coastal areas with bayberry and wax myrtle, including Cape Romain National Wildlife Refuge and Huntington Beach State Park.

Other ID: *Breeding Myrtle Warbler male:* white throat; yellow rump and shoulder patch; yellow cap; black streaking on chest. *Breeding Myrtle Warbler female:* similar to breeding male but lacks yellow cap.
Size: L 5½ in; W 9¼ in.
Voice: male's song is a brief, bubbling warble rising or falling at the end.
Status: abundant migrant and winter resident; less common in winter in the Mountains.
Habitat: well-vegetated habitats in lowlands, especially wax myrtle thickets.

Similar Birds

Black-throated
Green Warbler

Cape May Warbler

Magnolia Warbler

pale throat

2 white wing bars

yellow rump

yellow shoulder patch

♂

nonbreeding

"*Myrtle Warbler*"

♀

streaked breast

Nesting: does not nest in South Carolina; nests in the western and northern U.S. and in Canada; in a crotch or on a horizontal limb in a conifer; cup nest is made of vegetation and spider silk; brown-blotched, buff-colored eggs are ⅝ × ½ in; female incubates 4–5 eggs for up to 13 days.

Did You Know?

This small warbler's habit of flitting near buildings to snatch spiders from their webs has earned it the nickname "Spider Bird."

Look For

Small puddles that form during or after rains often attract warblers, allowing a good look at these secretive birds.

Yellow-throated Warbler

Dendroica dominica

The striking Yellow-throated Warbler is a breeding bird in the southeastern U.S. It is fond of wet, lowland forests and shows a preference for the upper canopy. In fact, this warbler forages more like a creeper than a warbler, inserting its unusually long bill into cracks and crevices in bark. Yellow-throated Warblers often forage on the undersides of horizontal branches and sometimes on the trunk, techniques also used by Black-and-white Warblers.

Other ID: black forehead; bold white underparts with black streaking on sides; 2 white wing bars.
Size: *L* 5–5½ in; *W* 8 in.
Voice: a series of downslurred whistles with a final rising note: *tee-ew tee-ew tee-ew tew-wee*.
Status: common breeder in the Coastal Plain and Piedmont; scarce in the Mountains in summer; uncommon winter resident in the Coastal Plain; common migrant throughout.
Habitat: primarily riparian woodlands with many tall sycamore trees; occasionally seen at backyard feeders in winter.

Similar Birds

Yellow-throated Vireo   Kentucky Warbler   Magnolia Warbler

white eyebrow
and ear patch

triangular,
black mask

bluish gray
upperparts

yellow throat
and upper
breast

♂

Nesting: high in a sycamore tree, often near a branch tip; female builds a cup nest of vegetation woven together with caterpillar silk; nest is lined with down and feathers; pale, speckled eggs are $5/8 \times 1/2$ in; female incubates 4 eggs for 12–13 days.

Did You Know?

This warbler sings a sweet, slow song, similar to a Yellow Warbler's *sweet sweet sweet, I am so sweet.*

Look For

The Yellow-throated Warbler can be found in bald cypress and sycamore forests, creeping along branches like a nuthatch.

Pine Warbler

Dendroica pinus

This unassuming bird is perfectly named because it is bound to South Carolina's majestic, sheltering pines. Pine Warblers are often difficult to find because they typically forage near the top of very tall, mature pine trees. They are particularly attracted to white pines and longleaf or loblolly pines and avoid species with shorter needles. • The Pine Warbler's modest appearance is very similar to a number of immature and fall-plumaged vireos and warblers, forcing birders to obtain a good, long look before making a positive identification. This warbler is most often confused with the Bay-breasted Warbler or Blackpoll Warbler in drab fall plumage.

Other ID: olive green head and back; dark grayish wings and tail; whitish to dusky wing bars; yellow throat and breast. *Female:* duller colors.
Size: L 5½ in; W 8¾ in.
Voice: song is a short, musical trill; call-note is a sweet *chip*.
Status: common resident, except in the Mountains where it is an uncommon breeder at lower elevations.
Habitat: mixed and deciduous woodlands.

Similar Birds

Prairie Warbler

Yellow-throated Vireo

faint, yellow, broken eye ring

faint, dark line through eye

♀

white undertail coverts and belly

♂

faded dark streaking or dusky wash on sides of breast

Nesting: near the end of a pine limb; deep, open cup nest of plant material and spider webs is lined with feathers; whitish, brown-speckled eggs are 1¾ × 1⅜ in; pair incubates 3–5 eggs for 12–13 days.

Did You Know?

Pine Warblers will visit bird feeders laden with peanut butter, nuts or cracked corn in winter.

Look For

In winter, these warblers join resident mixed flocks with chickadees, titmice and nuthatches, traveling together through the pine forests of South Carolina.

Common Yellowthroat

Geothlypis trichas

The bumblebee colors of the male Common Yellowthroat's black mask and yellow throat identify this skulking wetland resident. He sings his witchety song from strategically chosen cattail perches that he visits in rotation, fiercely guarding his territory against the intrusion of other males. The female has no mask and remains mostly hidden from view in thick vegetation when she tends to the nest.

Other ID: black bill; orangy legs. *Female:* may show faint, white eye ring.
Size: *L* 5 in; *W* 7 in.
Voice: song is a clear, oscillating *witchety witchety witchety-witch;* call is a sharp *tcheck* or *tchet.*
Status: common breeder; in winter, common at the coast but uncommon in the Mountains and Piedmont; common migrant statewide.
Habitat: cattail marshes, sedge wetlands, riparian areas, beaver ponds and wet, overgrown meadows; sometimes dry fields.

Similar Birds

Kentucky Warbler

Hooded Warbler
(p. 194)

Wilson's Warbler

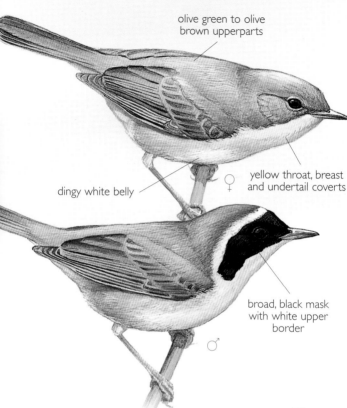

olive green to olive brown upperparts

dingy white belly

yellow throat, breast and undertail coverts

♀

broad, black mask with white upper border

♂

Nesting: on or near the ground or in a small shrub or emergent vegetation; female builds an open cup nest of weeds, grass, bark strips and moss; brown-blotched, white eggs are ⅝ × ½ in; female incubates 3–5 eggs for 12 days.

Did You Know?

Famous Swedish biologist Carolus Linnaeus named the Common Yellowthroat in 1766, making it one of the first North American birds to be recorded.

Look For

Common Yellowthroats immerse themselves or roll in water to bathe, then shake off the excess water by flicking or flapping their wings.

Hooded Warbler

Wilsonia citrina

Despite nesting low to the ground, Hooded Warblers require extensive mature forests, where fallen trees have opened gaps in the canopy, encouraging under-story growth. • Different species of wood-warblers can coexist in a limited environment because they partition their food supplies, with each species foraging exclusively in certain areas. Hooded Warblers also partition between the sexes: males tend to forage in treetops, while females forage near the ground.

Other ID: olive green upperparts; white undertail; pinkish legs. *Female:* yellow face and olive crown; may show faint traces of black hood.
Size: *L* 5½ in; *W* 7 in.
Voice: clear, whistling song is some variation of *whitta-witta-wit-tee-yo;* call note is a metallic *tink.*
Status: common breeder in the Mountains and the Coastal Plain, less common in the Piedmont; common migrant statewide.
Habitat: openings with dense, low shrubs in mature upland decid-uous and mixed forests; occasionally in moist ravines or mature white pine plantations with a dense understory of deciduous shrubs.

Similar Birds

Kentucky Warbler

Common Yellowthroat
(p. 192)

Wilson's Warbler

♀

black hood

♂

bright yellow
face

bright yellow
underparts

Nesting: low in a deciduous shrub; mostly the
female builds an open cup nest of fine plant
material, animal hair and spiderwebs; creamy
white, brown-spotted eggs are ⅝ × ½ in; female
incubates 4 eggs for about 12 days.

Did You Know?

In winter, males and
females segregate: males
use mature forest and
females use shrubby, dis-
turbed sites.

Look For

These warblers can be found
in wooded areas, including
pine forests with a shrubby
understory of blueberry or
laurel.

Summer Tanager

Piranga rubra

The Summer Tanager is a treat for southern birders—most of North America gets a glimpse of these beauties only if a rare individual flies off-track. This striking bird breeds throughout our forested areas, favoring the edges of pine or pine-oak forests and riparian areas. • Summer Tanagers thrive on a wide variety of insects, but they are best known for their practice of snatching flying bees and wasps from menacing swarms. They may even harass the occupants of a wasp nest until the nest is abandoned and the larvae inside are left free for the picking.

Other ID: immature male has patchy, red and greenish plumage.

Size: *L* 7–8 in; *W* 12 in.

Voice: song is a series of 3–5 sweet, clear, whistled phrases; call is a *pit* or *pit-a-tuck*.

Status: common breeder in the Piedmont and Coastal Plain; uncommon at low elevations in the Mountains; uncommon migrant at lower elevations statewide.

Habitat: mixed coniferous and deciduous woodlands, or riparian woodlands with cottonwoods; occasionally in wooded backyards.

Similar Birds

Scarlet Tanager

Northern Cardinal
(p. 208)

Orchard Oriole
(p. 222), female

thick, pale bill

varies from overall grayish yellow to greenish with reddish wash

small crest

rose red overall

♀

♂

Nesting: constructed on a high, horizontal tree limb; female builds a flimsy, shallow cup of grass, Spanish moss and twigs and lines it with fine grass; pale blue-green eggs, spotted with reddish brown are ⅞ × ⅝ in; female incubates 3–4 eggs for 11–12 days.

Did You Know?

The male Summer Tanager keeps his rosy red plumage all year, unlike the male Scarlet Tanager, which molts to a greenish yellow plumage in fall.

Look For

A courting male tanager will hop persistently in front of or over the female while offering her food and fanning his handsome crest and tail feathers.

Eastern Towhee
Pipilo erythrophthalmus

Eastern Towhees are large, colorful members of the sparrow family. These noisy birds are often heard before they are seen as they rustle about in dense undergrowth, craftily scraping back layers of dry leaves to expose the seeds, berries or insects hidden beneath. They employ an unusual two-footed technique to uncover food items—a strategy that is especially important in winter when virtually all of their food is taken from the ground. • The Eastern Towhee and its western relative, the Spotted Towhee *(P. maculata)*, were once grouped together as the "Rufous-sided Towhee."

Other ID: white lower breast and belly; buff under-tail coverts; eyes commonly red, but in the south-eastern U.S. may be white or orange. *In flight:* white outer tail corners.
Size: *L* 7–8½ in; *W* 10½ in.
Voice: song is 2 high, whistled notes followed by a trill: *drink your teeeee;* call is a scratchy, slurred *cheweee!* or *chewink!*
Status: common permanent resident.
Habitat: along woodland edges and in shrubby, abandoned fields.

Similar Birds

Dark-eyed Junco
(p. 206)

Orchard Oriole
(p. 222), male

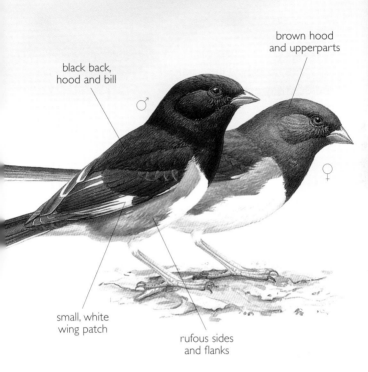

brown hood
and upperparts

black back,
hood and bill

♂

♀

small, white
wing patch

rufous sides
and flanks

Nesting: on the ground or low in a dense shrub;
female builds a cup nest of twigs, bark strips,
grass and animal hair; pale, brown-spotted,
creamy eggs are ⅞ × ⅝ in; mainly the female
incubates 3–4 eggs for 12–13 days.

Did You Know?

The scientific name
Erythrophthalmus means
"red eye" in Greek, though
towhees in the southeast-
ern states may have white
or orange irises.

Look For

Showy towhees are easily
attracted to feeders, where
they scratch on the ground
for millet, oats or sunflower
seeds.

Field Sparrow

Spizella pusilla

This gentle bird breeds throughout our state, concealing a delicate nest near the ground, among bushes or in clumps of tall grass. • The Field Sparrow has learned to recognize when its nest has been parasitized by the Brown-headed Cowbird. Because the unwelcome eggs are usually too large for this small sparrow to eject, the nest is simply abandoned and a new nest is built elsewhere.

Other ID: 2 white wing bars; pinkish legs.
Rufous morph: rusty streak behind eye; buffy red wash on breast, sides and flanks. *Gray morph:* gray head and underparts.
Size: L 5–6 in; W 8 in.
Voice: song is a series of woeful, musical, downslurred whistles accelerating into a trill.
Status: fairly common breeder in the Coastal Plain and Mountains; common breeder in the Piedmont; common winter visitor.
Habitat: abandoned or weedy and overgrown fields and pastures, woodland edges and clearings, extensive shrubby riparian areas and young conifer plantations.

Similar Birds

Chipping Sparrow

Vesper Sparrow

Grasshopper Sparrow

rusty crown with
gray central stripe

white
eye ring

large, orange-
pink bill

rufous morph

gray or buffy
unstreaked
underparts

Nesting: on or near the ground, often sheltered by a shrub; female weaves an open cup
nest of grass and lines it with soft material;
brown-spotted, whitish to pale bluish eggs
are ¾ × ½ in; female incubates 3–5 eggs for
10–12 days.

Did You Know?

In fall, hundreds of Field
Sparrows may crowd into
weedy fields to feed.

Look For

A pink bill and rusty head can
help to distinguish the Field
Sparrow from similar small,
brown birds.

Seaside Sparrow
Ammodramus maritimus

The Seaside Sparrow is one of the most variable species in South Carolina, represented by several different races. A few of these races previously were considered separate species. • Seaside Sparrows are a uniquely American species, being permanent residents discontinuously from New Hampshire to Texas, with only casual records to extreme southeastern Canada. Some northern birds migrate south in winter as well. • Foraging primarily on the ground, this stocky, little bird enjoys a diverse diet of insects, spiders, small aquatic invertebrates and seeds.

Other ID: dark, variable plumage; white throat.
Size: *L* 6 in; *W* 7½ in.
Voice: complex song typically ends with a buzz: *chup teedle tzeeee;* call is a low *chup.*
Status: fairly common breeder in summer; common in winter in coastal marshes.
Habitat: coastal marshes.

Similar Birds

Swamp Sparrow

Saltmarsh Sharp-tailed Sparrow

Nelson's Sharp-tailed Sparrow

dusky head

yellow lores

upperparts including nape and crown are dusky with blackish stripes

white "mustache"

underparts dusky with indistinct streaking

Nesting: in marsh vegetation, 8–10 in above the ground; female builds a cup nest of grass and rushes, lined with finer materials; brown-speckled, pale greenish white eggs are ⅞ × ⅝ in; female incubates 4–5 eggs for 11–12 days.

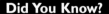

Did You Know?

Seaside Sparrows can be used to indicate the health of coastal marshes, because they depend on this specific habitat and are sensitive to changes.

Look For

Your best chance of meeting this secretive bird is on tidal salt marshes where tall stands of marsh grass, rushes and shrubs provide a perfect habitat.

White-throated Sparrow

Zonotrichia albicollis

The White-throated Sparrow's distinctive song makes it one of the easiest sparrows to learn and identify. Its familiar bold, white throat and striped crown can be confused with only the White-crowned Sparrow *(Z. leucophrys),* but White-throats usually stick to forested woodlands, whereas White-crowns prefer open, bushy habitats and farmlands. • Two color morphs are common: one has black and white stripes on the head; the other has brown and tan stripes. These two color morphs are perpetuated because each morph almost always breeds with the opposite color morph.

Other ID: head may have brown and tan stripes; unstreaked, gray underparts; mottled brown upperparts.
Size: L 6½–7½ in; W 9 in.
Voice: variable song is a clear, distinct, whistled *Old Sam Peabody, Peabody, Peabody;* call is a sharp *chink.*
Status: common winter resident.
Habitat: woodlots, wooded parks and riparian brush.

Similar Birds

White-crowned
Sparrow

Swamp Sparrow

black-and-white-striped head

grayish bill

yellow lores

white throat

white-striped morph

Nesting: does not nest in South Carolina; nests in the Great Lakes region and throughout Canada; on or near the ground, often concealed by a low shrub or fallen log; open cup nest of plant material is lined with fine grass and hair; bluish, spotted eggs are ⅞ × ½ in; female incubates 4–5 eggs for 11–14 days.

Did You Know?

Zonotrichia means "hair-like," a reference to the striped heads of birds in this genus.

Look For

Urban backyards dressed with brushy fenceline tangles and a bird feeder brimming with seeds can attract good numbers of these delightful sparrows.

Dark-eyed Junco

Junco hyemalis

Juncos usually congregate in backyards with bird feeders and sheltering conifers—with such amenities at their disposal, more and more juncos are appearing in urban areas. These birds spend most of their time on the ground, snatching up seeds underneath bird feeders, and they are readily flushed from wooded trails and backyard feeders. Their distinctive, white outer tail feathers flash in alarm as they seek cover in a nearby tree or shrub. • The junco is often called the "Snow Bird," and the species name, *hyemalis,* means "winter" in Greek.

Other ID: *Female:* gray-brown where male is slate gray.
Size: *L* 6–7 in; *W* 9 in.
Voice: song is a long, dry trill; call is a smacking *chip* note, often given in series.
Status: limited breeder in the Mountains; common winter resident.
Habitat: shrubby woodland borders, backyard feeders.

Similar Birds

Eastern Towhee
(p. 198)

Look For

The resident breeding subspecies has a darker gray bill whereas the more northern subspecies that migrates here in winter has a pinkish bill.

pale pink bill

dark slate gray
upperparts

♂

white outer
tail feathers

white belly and
undertail coverts

"Slate-colored Junco"

Nesting: on the ground, usually concealed; female builds a cup nest of twigs, grass, bark shreds and moss; brown-marked, whitish to bluish eggs are ¾ × ½ in; female incubates 3–5 eggs for 12–13 days.

Did You Know?

There are five closely related Dark-eyed Junco subspecies in North America that share similar habits but differ in coloration and range. The "Slate-colored Junco" is the subspecies that is widespread and common in eastern North America.

Northern Cardinal

Cardinalis cardinalis

A male Northern Cardinal will display his unforget-table, vibrant red head crest and raise his tail when he is excited or agitated. The male will vigorously defend his territory, even attacking his own reflection in a window or hubcap! • Cardinals are one of only a few bird species to maintain strong pair bonds. Some couples sing to each other year-round, while others join loose flocks. Pair bonds are reestablished in spring during a "courtship feeding": the male offers a seed to the female, which she then accepts and eats.

Other ID: *Male:* red overall. *Female:* brownish buff overall; fainter mask; red crest, wings and tail.
Size: *L* 8–9 in; *W* 12 in.
Voice: call is a metallic *chip;* song is series of clear, bubbly whistled notes: *What cheer! What cheer! birdie-birdie-birdie what cheer!*
Status: common permanent resident.
Habitat: brushy thickets and shrubby tangles along forest and woodland edges; backyards and urban and suburban parks.

Similar Birds

Summer Tanager
(p. 196)

Scarlet Tanager

pointed crest

red,
conical bill

♀

♂

black mask
and throat

Nesting: in a dense shrub, vine tangle or low in a coniferous tree; female builds an open cup nest of twigs, grass and bark shreds; brown-blotched, white to greenish white eggs are 1 × ¾ in; female incubates 3–4 eggs for 12–13 days.

Did You Know?

This bird owes its name to the vivid red plumage of the male, which resembles the robes of Roman Catholic cardinals.

Look For

Northern Cardinals fly with jerky movements and short glides and have a preference for sunflower seeds.

Indigo Bunting
Passerina cyanea

The vivid, electric blue male Indigo Bunting is one of the most spectacular birds in South Carolina. The male is a persistent singer, vocalizing even through the heat of a summer day. A young male doesn't learn his couplet song from his parents but rather from neighboring males during his first year on his own. • These birds arrive in April or May and favor raspberry thickets as nest sites. Dense, thorny stems keep most predators at a distance, and the berries are a good food source. • Planting coneflowers, cosmos or foxtail grasses may attract Indigo Buntings to your backyard.

Other ID: no wing bars. *Male:* bright blue overall; black lores. *Female:* soft brown overall; whitish throat.
Size: L 5½ in; W 8 in.
Voice: song consists of paired warbled whistles: *fire-fire, where-where, here-here, see-it see-it;* call is a quick *spit.*
Status: common breeder; abundant fall migrant.
Habitat: deciduous forest and woodland edges, regenerating forest clearings, orchards and shrubby fields.

Similar Birds

Blue Grosbeak

Eastern Bluebird
(p. 168)

♂

darker blue head

gray, conical bill

faint brown
streaks on breast

breeding ♀

wings and tail
may show
some black

Nesting: in a small tree, shrub or within a vine tangle; female builds a cup nest of grass, leaves and bark strips; unmarked, white to bluish white eggs are ¾ × ½ in; female incubates 3–4 eggs for 12–13 days.

Did You Know?

Females choose the most melodious males as mates, because these males can usually establish territories with the finest habitat.

Look For

The Indigo Bunting will land midway on a stem of grass or on a weed and shuffle slowly toward the seed head, bending down the stem to reach the seeds.

Painted Bunting
Passerina ciris

The stunning male Painted Bunting wears almost every color of the rainbow and graces southern thickets with his sweet songs. Although not nearly as unmistakable as an adult male, the female is still attractive: her plumage is a rich greenish above and pale yellow below. Unlike some other songbirds, the adult male Painted Bunting retains his bright colors during winter. • Song battles occasionally escalate to physical fights when two male Painted Buntings argue over territory ownership or boundaries.

Other ID: *Female:* brilliant yellow-green above and pale yellow below; yellow orbital ring. *Juveniles:* similar to females but duller, more grayish green.
Size: L 5½ in; W 8¾ in.
Voice: song is a sweet, clear series of warbling notes; call is a sharp *chip*.
Status: fairly common breeder on the immediate coastal region and inland a little farther south.
Habitat: breeds in shrubby fields, hammock edges and citrus groves; may overwinter in backyards with much cover.

Look For

Though most common along the coast from mid-April to October, a few Painted Buntings overwinter at South Carolina bird feeders each year. They prefer offerings of sunflower seeds or seed mixes.

brilliant blue head with
red orbital ring

greenish yellow
back and wings

♀

♂

wholly red
underparts
including throat

Nesting: in a shrub or low tree; female weaves
an open cup from grass, weed stems and leaves
lined with fine plant material and animal hair;
finely speckled, white eggs are ¾ × ½ in; female
incubates 3–4 eggs for 11–12 days; usually
double-brooded.

Did You Know?

Painted Buntings have two separate breeding ranges: along
the Atlantic coast from South Carolina to Florida, and mostly
inland from Alabama to Mexico. The smaller Atlantic Coast
breeding population is declining in numbers, mostly because
of increased brood parasitism from Brown-headed Cowbirds
and coastal development.

Red-winged Blackbird
Agelaius phoeniceus

The male Red-winged Blackbird wears his bright red shoulders like armor—together with his short, raspy song, they are key in defending his territory from rivals. In field experiments, males whose red shoulders were painted black soon lost their territories. • Nearly every cattail marsh worthy of note in South Carolina hosts Red-winged Blackbirds during at least some of the year.

Other ID: *Male:* black overall. *Female:* mottled brown upperparts; pale eyebrow.
Size: L 7½–9 in; W 13 in.
Voice: song is a loud, raspy *konk-a-ree* or *ogle-reeeee;* calls include a harsh *check* and high *tseert;* female gives a loud *che-che-che chee chee chee.*
Status: common breeder; abundant winter visitor especially at the coast.
Habitat: cattail marshes, wet meadows and ditches, croplands and shoreline shrubs.

Similar Birds

Common Grackle   Rusty Blackbird   Brown-headed Cowbird (p. 220)

red shoulder patch
is edged in yellow

♂

faint, red
shoulder
patch

♀

heavily streaked
underparts

Nesting: colonial; in cattails or shoreline bushes; female builds an open cup nest of dried cattail leaves lined with fine grass; darkly marked, pale bluish green eggs are 1 × ¾ in; female incubates 3–4 eggs for 10–12 days.

Did You Know?

Some scientists believe that the Red-winged Blackbird is the most abundant bird species in North America.

Look For

As he sings his *konk-a-ree* song, the male Red-winged Blackbird spreads his shoulders to display his bright red wing patch to rivals and potential mates.

Eastern Meadowlark
Sturnella magna

The drab dress of most female songbirds lends them protection during the breeding season, but the female Eastern Meadowlark uses a different strategy. Her V-shaped "necklace" and bright yellow throat and belly create a colorful distraction that leads predators away from the nest. A female flushed from the nest while incubating her eggs will often abandon the nest. Though she will never abandon her chicks, she will be extra careful to not reveal the location of her nest, which usually results in less frequent feeding of nestlings.

Other ID: yellow underparts; mottled brown upperparts; long, sharp bill; long, pinkish legs. *Nonbreeding:* paler breastband and flank streaks.

Size: *L* 9–9½ in; *W* 14 in.

Voice: song is a rich series of 2–8 melodic, clear, slurred whistles: *see-you at school-today* or *this is the year;* gives a rattling flight call.

Status: fairly common permanent resident; less common in winter in the Mountains.

Habitat: grassy meadows and pastures, some croplands, weedy fields, grassy roadsides and old orchards; also coastal barrens in migration and winter.

Similar Birds

Dickcissel

Look For

The Eastern Meadowlark often whistles its proud song from fence posts and power lines.

yellow lore

white jaw line

broad, black breast band

dark streaking on white sides and flanks

short, wide tail with white outer feathers

breeding

Nesting: in a concealed depression on the ground; female builds a domed grass nest, woven into surrounding vegetation; heavily spotted, white eggs are 1⅛ × ¾ in; female incubates 3–7 eggs for 13–15 days.

Did You Know?

This bird likely got its name because its song reminded early settlers of the song of the Skylark (*Alauda arvensis*) of Europe. But the Eastern Meadowlark is not a lark at all—it is actually a brightly colored member of the blackbird family. Its silhouette reveals its blackbird features.

Boat-tailed Grackle

Quiscalus major

Feathers fluffed, tail spread and wings fluttering above its back, the Boat-tailed Grackle issues harsh, grating calls across the marsh landscape. • Bold and seemingly carefree, the Boat-tailed Grackle has been known to eat eggs from the unguarded nests of other birds, including much larger species such as herons and rails. This grackle is closely associated with coastal waters, where it wades through the shallows or walks on top of floating vegetation while searching for snails and mussels.

Other ID: yellow eyes; long, keel-shaped tail. *Female:* orangy brown underparts; brown mask and crown; darker wings and tail.
Size: *Male:* L 16½ in; W 23 in. *Female:* L 14 in; W 17½ in.
Voice: song consists of harsh *jeeb* notes repeated in series.
Status: common permanent resident on the immediate coast.
Habitat: saltwater marshes, beaches, mudflats and other oceanside habitats; rarely inland near large lakes in the Coastal Plain.

Similar Birds

Common Grackle   Brewer's Blackbird

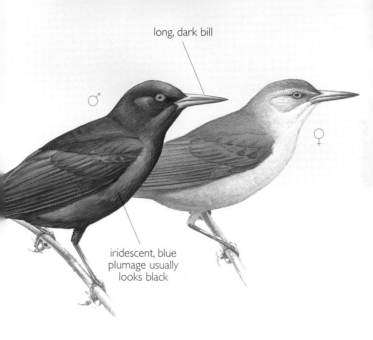

long, dark bill

♂

♀

iridescent, blue
plumage usually
looks black

Nesting: colonial; in vegetation at the edge of
a marsh or other water body; female builds
bulky cup nest from marsh vegetation and mud;
darkly scrawled, pale blue eggs are 1¼ × ⅞ in;
female incubates 2–3 eggs for 12–14 days.

Did You Know?

The Boat-tailed Grackle
and the similar Great-
tailed Grackle of the south-
west were, until the 1970s,
considered to be the same
species.

Look For

If an intruder enters the
aggressively guarded breeding
territory, the male grackle
points his bill skyward in
a threatening posture that
warns of an impending attack.

Brown-headed Cowbird
Molothrus ater

These nomads historically followed bison herds across the Great Plains (they now follow cattle), so they never stayed in one area long enough to build and tend a nest. Instead, cowbirds lay their eggs in other birds' nests, relying on the unsuspecting adoptive parents to incubate the eggs and feed the aggressive young. Orioles, warblers, vireos and tanagers are among the most affected species. Increased livestock farming and fragmentation of forests has encouraged the expansion of the cowbird's range. It is known to parasitize more than 140 bird species.

Other ID: dark eyes; thick, conical bill; short, squared tail.
Size: *L* 6–8 in; *W* 12 in.
Voice: song is a high, liquidy gurgle: *glug-ahl-whee* or *bubbloozeee*.
Status: common permanent resident; abundant along the coast in winter.
Habitat: agricultural and residential areas and areas near cattle.

Similar Birds

Rusty Blackbird

Red-winged Blackbird
(p. 214)

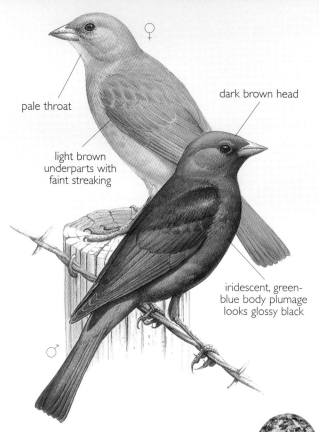

pale throat

dark brown head

light brown underparts with faint streaking

iridescent, green-blue body plumage looks glossy black

♀

♂

Nesting: does not build a nest; female lays up to 30 eggs a year in the nests of other birds, usually 1 egg per nest; brown-speckled, whitish eggs are ⅞ × ⅝ in; eggs hatch after 10–13 days.

Did You Know?

When courting a female, the male cowbird points his bill upward to the sky, fans his tail and wings and utters a loud squeak.

Look For

When cowbirds feed in flocks, they hold their back ends up high, with their tails sticking straight up in the air.

Orchard Oriole

Icterus spurius

Orchards may once have been favored haunts of this oriole, but since orchards are now heavily sprayed and manicured, it is unlikely that you will ever see this bird in such a locale. Instead, the Orchard Oriole is most commonly found in large shade trees that line roads, paths and streams. • Smaller than all other North American orioles, the Orchard Oriole is one of only two oriole species commonly found in the eastern United States. • In some parts of its breeding range, over half of the Orchard Oriole nests are parasitized by cowbirds.

Other ID: *Female* and *immature:* olive upperparts; yellow to olive yellow underparts; faint, white wing bars on dusky gray wings.
Size: *L* 6–7 in; *W* 9½ in.
Voice: song is a loud, rapid, varied series of whistled notes; call is a quick *chuck*.
Status: common breeder in the Piedmont and Coastal Plain; less common breeder in the Mountains; very rare at the coast in winter.
Habitat: open woodlands, suburban parklands, forest edges, hedgerows and groves of shade trees.

Similar Birds

Baltimore Oriole

Summer Tanager
(p. 196)

American Robin
(p. 172)

black hood and tail

♂

♀

dark wings with
white wing bar and
feather edgings

chestnut
underparts,
shoulder and
rump

Nesting: in the fork of a deciduous tree or
shrub; female builds a hanging pouch nest woven
from grass and plant fibers; pale bluish white,
sparsely marked eggs are ¾ × ½ in; female incubates 4–5 eggs for about 12–15 days.

Did You Know?

The Orchard Oriole is
one of the first species to
migrate following breeding
and is usually absent by
the beginning of August.

Look For

Orchard Orioles are best
seen in spring when eager
males hop from branch to
branch, singing their quick,
musical courtship songs.

House Finch
Carpodacus mexicanus

A native to western North America, the House Finch was brought to eastern parts of the continent as an illegally captured cage bird known as the "Hollywood Finch." In the early 1940s, New York pet shop owners released their birds to avoid prosecution and fines, and it is likely the descendants of those birds that have colonized our area. In fact, the House Finch is now commonly found throughout the continental U.S. and has been introduced in Hawaii. • Only the resourceful House Finch has been aggressive and stubborn enough to successfully outcompete the House Sparrow.

Other ID: streaked undertail coverts. *Female:* indistinct facial patterning; heavily streaked underparts.
Size: L 5–6 in; W 9½ in.
Voice: song is a bright, disjointed warble lasting about 3 seconds, often ending with a harsh *jeeer* or *wheer;* flight call is a sweet *cheer,* given singly or in series.
Status: becoming a common permanent resident statewide.
Habitat: cities, towns and agricultural areas.

Similar Birds

Purple Finch

Pine Siskin

short bill with curved upper bill

bright red eyebrow, forecrown, throat and breast

brown-streaked back

heavily streaked flanks

♀

♂

square tail

Nesting: in a cavity, building, dense foliage or abandoned bird nest; open cup nest of plants and other debris; pale blue, spotted eggs are ¾ × ½ in; female incubates 4–5 eggs for 12–14 days.

Did You Know?

The male House Finch's plumage varies in color from light yellow to bright red, but females will choose the reddest males with which to breed.

Look For

In flight, the House Finch has a square tail, while the similar looking Purple Finch has a sharply notched tail.

American Goldfinch
Carduelis tristis

Like vibrant rays of sunshine, American Goldfinches cheerily flutter over weedy fields and gardens and along roadsides. It is hard to miss their jubilant *po-ta-to-chip* call and their distinctive, undulating flight style. • Because these acrobatic birds regularly feed while hanging upside down, finch feeders are designed with the seed-openings below the perches. These feeders discourage the more aggressive House Sparrows, which feed upright, from stealing the seeds. Use niger or black oil sunflower seeds to attract American Goldfinches to your bird feeder.

Other ID: *Nonbreeding:* olive brown overall; dark bill; black wings and tail; pale wing bars; white undertail coverts; male has yellow wash on face.
Size: *L* 4½–5 in; *W* 9 in.
Voice: song is a long, varied series of trills, twitters, warbles and hissing notes; calls include *po-ta-to-chip* or *per-chic-or-ee* (often delivered in flight) and a whistled *dear-me, see-me*.
Status: locally common to fairly common breeder and winter resident.
Habitat: weedy fields, woodland edges, meadows, riparian areas, parks and gardens.

Similar Birds

Evening Grosbeak   Wilson's Warbler

yellow-green upperparts

black cap extends onto forehead

black wings with white wing bars

♀

♂

white rump and under-tail coverts

breeding

Nesting: in the fork of a deciduous tree; compact cup nest of plant fibers, grass and spider silk; pale bluish eggs are ⅝ × ½ in; female incubates 4–6 eggs for 12–14 days.

Did You Know?

These birds nest in late summer to ensure that there is a dependable source of seeds to feed their young.

Look For

American Goldfinches delight in perching on late-summer thistle heads or poking through dandelion patches in search of seeds.

House Sparrow
Passer domesticus

A black mask and "bib" adorn the male of this adaptive, aggressive species. The House Sparrow's tendency to usurp territory has led to a decline in native bird populations. This sparrow will even help itself to the convenience of another bird's home, such as a bluebird or Cliff Swallow nest or a Purple Martin house. • This abundant and conspicuous bird was introduced to North America in the 1850s as part of a plan to control the insects that were damaging grain and cereal crops. As it turns out, these birds are largely vegetarian!

Other ID: *Breeding male:* gray crown; black bill; dark, mottled upperparts; gray underparts; white wing bar. *Female:* indistinct facial patterns; plain gray-brown overall; streaked upperparts.
Size: *L* 5½–6½ in; *W* 9½ in.
Voice: song is a plain, familiar *cheep-cheep-cheep-cheep;* call is a short *chill-up.*
Status: abundant permanent resident.
Habitat: townsites, urban and suburban areas, farmyards and agricultural areas, railroad yards and other developed areas.

Similar Birds

Indigo Bunting
(p. 210), female

Look For

In spring, House Sparrows feast on the buds of fruit trees and will sometimes even eat lettuce from backyard gardens!

buffy eyebrow

grayish, unstreaked underparts

chestnut nape

black lores and "bib"

light gray cheek

♀

♂

breeding

Nesting: often communal; in a birdhouse, ornamental shrub or natural cavity; pair builds a large dome nest of grass, twigs and plant fibers; gray-speckled, white to greenish eggs are ⅞ × ⅝ in; pair incubates 4–6 eggs for 10–13 days.

Did You Know?

House Sparrows have a high reproductive output—a pair may raise up to four clutches per year, with up to seven young per clutch. When you consider this, it is easier to understand how the species spread to cover most of North America in such a short period of time!

Glossary

brood: *n.* a family of young from one hatching; *v.* to sit on eggs so as to hatch them.

buteo: a high-soaring hawk (genus *Buteo*); characterized by broad wings and short, wide tails; feeds mostly on small mammals and other land animals.

cere: a fleshy area at the base of a bird's bill that contains the nostrils.

clutch: the number of eggs laid by the female at one time.

corvid: a member of the crow family (Corvidae); includes crows, jays, ravens and magpies.

covey: a group of birds, usually grouse or quail.

crop: an enlargement of the esophagus; serves as a storage structure and (in pigeons) has glands that produce secretions.

dabbling: a foraging technique used by ducks, in which the head and neck are submerged but the body and tail remain on the water's surface; dabbling ducks can usually walk easily on land, can take off without running and have brightly colored speculums.

eclipse plumage: a cryptic plumage, similar to that of females, worn by some male ducks in autumn when they molt their flight feathers and consequently are unable to fly.

endangered: a species that is facing extirpation or extinction in all or part of its range.

extirpated: a species that no longer exists in the wild in a particular region but occurs elsewhere.

fledge: to leave the nest for the first time.

fledgling: a young bird that has left the nest but is dependent upon its parents.

flushing: a behavior in which frightened birds explode into flight in response to a disturbance.

flycatching: a feeding behavior in which the bird leaves a perch, snatches an insect in midair and then returns to the same perch.

hawking: attempting to catch insects through aerial pursuit.

leading edge: the front edge of the wing as viewed from below.

mantle: feathers of the back and upperside of folded wings.

molt: the periodic shedding and regrowth of worn feathers (often twice per year).

morph: one of several alternate plumages displayed by members of a species.

primaries: the outermost flight feathers.

riparian: refers to habitat along riverbanks.

rufous: rusty red in color.

speculum: a brightly colored patch on the wings of many dabbling ducks.

vagrant: a transient bird found outside its normal range.

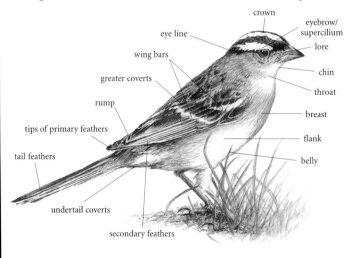

Checklist

The following checklist contains 396 species of birds that have been officially recorded as definitive in South Carolina. Species are grouped by family and listed in taxonomic order in accordance with the A.O.U. *Checklist of North American Birds* (7th ed.) and its supplements. In addition, the following risk categories are also noted: endangered (en) and threatened (th).

We wish to thank the Carolina Bird Club for their kind assistance in providing the information for this checklist.

Waterfowl
❏ Fulvous Whistling-Duck
❏ Black-bellied Whistling-Duck
❏ Greater White-fronted Goose
❏ Snow Goose
❏ Ross's Goose
❏ Canada Goose
❏ Brant
❏ Tundra Swan
❏ Wood Duck
❏ Gadwall
❏ Eurasian Wigeon
❏ American Wigeon
❏ American Black Duck
❏ Mallard
❏ Mottled Duck
❏ Blue-winged Teal
❏ Cinnamon Teal
❏ Northern Shoveler
❏ Northern Pintail
❏ Green-winged Teal
❏ Canvasback
❏ Redhead
❏ Ring-necked Duck
❏ Greater Scaup
❏ Lesser Scaup
❏ King Eider
❏ Common Eider
❏ Surf Scoter
❏ White-winged Scoter
❏ Black Scoter
❏ Long-tailed Duck
❏ Bufflehead
❏ Common Goldeneye
❏ Hooded Merganser
❏ Common Merganser
❏ Red-breasted Merganser
❏ Ruddy Duck

Grouse & Allies
❏ Ruffed Grouse
❏ Wild Turkey

Quail
❏ Northern Bobwhite

Loons
❏ Red-throated Loon
❏ Common Loon

Grebes
❏ Pied-billed Grebe
❏ Horned Grebe
❏ Red-necked Grebe
❏ Eared Grebe
❏ Western Grebe

Fulmars, Petrels & Shearwaters
❏ Northern Fulmar
❏ Black-capped Petrel

❏ Cory's Shearwater
❏ Greater Shearwater
❏ Sooty Shearwater
❏ Manx Shearwater
❏ Audubon's Shearwater
❏ Little Shearwater

Storm-Petrels
❏ Wilson's Storm-Petrel
❏ Leach's Storm-Petrel
❏ Band-rumped Storm-Petrel

Tropicbirds
❏ White-tailed Tropicbird
❏ Red-billed Tropicbird

Boobies & Gannets
❏ Masked Booby
❏ Brown Booby
❏ Red-footed Booby
❏ Northern Gannet

Pelicans
❏ American White Pelican
❏ Brown Pelican

Cormorants
❏ Double-crested Cormorant
❏ Great Cormorant

Darters
❏ Anhinga

Frigatebirds
❏ Magnificent Frigatebird

Herons & Egrets
❏ American Bittern
❏ Least Bittern
❏ Great Blue Heron
❏ Great Egret
❏ Snowy Egret
❏ Little Blue Heron
❏ Tricolored Heron
❏ Reddish Egret
❏ Cattle Egret
❏ Green Heron
❏ Black-crowned Night-Heron
❏ Yellow-crowned Night-Heron

Ibises & Spoonbills
❏ White Ibis

❏ Glossy Ibis
❏ Roseate Spoonbill

Storks
❏ Wood Stork (en)

Vultures
❏ Black Vulture
❏ Turkey Vulture

Kites, Hawks & Eagles
❏ Osprey
❏ Swallow-tailed Kite
❏ White-tailed Kite
❏ Mississippi Kite
❏ Bald Eagle (th)
❏ Northern Harrier
❏ Sharp-shinned Hawk
❏ Cooper's Hawk
❏ Red-shouldered Hawk
❏ Broad-winged Hawk
❏ Red-tailed Hawk
❏ Golden Eagle

Falcons
❏ American Kestrel
❏ Merlin
❏ Peregrine Falcon

Rails & Allies
❏ Yellow Rail
❏ Black Rail
❏ Clapper Rail
❏ King Rail
❏ Virginia Rail
❏ Sora
❏ Purple Gallinule
❏ Common Moorhen
❏ American Coot

Limpkins
❏ Limpkin

Cranes
❏ Sandhill Crane
❏ Whooping Crane

Plovers
❏ Black-bellied Plover
❏ American Golden-Plover
❏ Snowy Plover
❏ Wilson's Plover

- ❑ Semipalmated Plover
- ❑ Piping Plover (th)
- ❑ Killdeer

Oystercatchers
- ❑ American Oystercatcher

Stilts & Avocets
- ❑ Black-necked Stilt
- ❑ American Avocet

Sandpipers & Allies
- ❑ Greater Yellowlegs
- ❑ Lesser Yellowlegs
- ❑ Solitary Sandpiper
- ❑ Willet
- ❑ Spotted Sandpiper
- ❑ Upland Sandpiper
- ❑ Whimbrel
- ❑ Long-billed Curlew
- ❑ Hudsonian Godwit
- ❑ Marbled Godwit
- ❑ Ruddy Turnstone
- ❑ Red Knot
- ❑ Sanderling
- ❑ Semipalmated Sandpiper
- ❑ Western Sandpiper
- ❑ Least Sandpiper
- ❑ White-rumped Sandpiper
- ❑ Baird's Sandpiper
- ❑ Pectoral Sandpiper
- ❑ Purple Sandpiper
- ❑ Dunlin
- ❑ Curlew Sandpiper
- ❑ Stilt Sandpiper
- ❑ Buff-breasted Sandpiper
- ❑ Ruff
- ❑ Short-billed Dowitcher
- ❑ Long-billed Dowitcher
- ❑ Wilson's Snipe
- ❑ American Woodcock
- ❑ Wilson's Phalarope
- ❑ Red-necked Phalarope
- ❑ Red Phalarope

Gulls & Allies
- ❑ Pomarine Jaeger
- ❑ Parasitic Jaeger
- ❑ Laughing Gull
- ❑ Franklin's Gull
- ❑ Black-headed Gull
- ❑ Bonaparte's Gull
- ❑ Ring-billed Gull
- ❑ Herring Gull
- ❑ Iceland Gull
- ❑ Lesser Black-backed Gull
- ❑ Glaucous Gull
- ❑ Great Black-backed Gull
- ❑ Sabine's Gull
- ❑ Black-legged Kittiwake
- ❑ Gull-billed Tern
- ❑ Caspian Tern
- ❑ Royal Tern
- ❑ Sandwich Tern
- ❑ Common Tern
- ❑ Forster's Tern
- ❑ Least Tern
- ❑ Bridled Tern
- ❑ Sooty Tern
- ❑ White-winged Tern
- ❑ Black Tern
- ❑ Brown Noddy
- ❑ Black Skimmer

Alcids
- ❑ Dovekie
- ❑ Thick-billed Murre
- ❑ Razorbill
- ❑ Black Guillemot
- ❑ Long-billed Murrelet

Pigeons & Doves
- ❑ Rock Pigeon
- ❑ Band-tailed Pigeon
- ❑ Eurasian Collared-Dove
- ❑ White-winged Dove
- ❑ Mourning Dove
- ❑ Common Ground-Dove

Parakeets
- ❑ Carolina Parakeet

Cuckoos & Anis
- ❑ Black-billed Cuckoo
- ❑ Yellow-billed Cuckoo
- ❑ Groove-billed Ani

Owls
- ❑ Barn Owl

❏ Eastern Screech-Owl
❏ Great Horned Owl
❏ Snowy Owl
❏ Burrowing Owl
❏ Barred Owl
❏ Long-eared Owl
❏ Short-eared Owl
❏ Northern Saw-whet Owl

Nightjars
❏ Common Nighthawk
❏ Chuck-will's-widow
❏ Whip-poor-will

Swifts
❏ Chimney Swift

Hummingbirds
❏ Buff-bellied Hummingbird
❏ Ruby-throated Hummingbird
❏ Black-chinned Hummingbird
❏ Calliope Hummingbird
❏ Rufous Hummingbird

Kingfishers
❏ Belted Kingfisher

Woodpeckers
❏ Red-headed Woodpecker
❏ Red-bellied Woodpecker
❏ Yellow-bellied Sapsucker
❏ Downy Woodpecker
❏ Hairy Woodpecker
❏ Red-cockaded Woodpecker (en)
❏ Northern Flicker
❏ Pileated Woodpecker

Flycatchers
❏ Olive-sided Flycatcher
❏ Eastern Wood-Pewee
❏ Yellow-bellied Flycatcher
❏ Acadian Flycatcher
❏ Willow Flycatcher
❏ Least Flycatcher
❏ Eastern Phoebe
❏ Vermilion Flycatcher
❏ Great Crested Flycatcher

❏ Western Kingbird
❏ Eastern Kingbird
❏ Gray Kingbird
❏ Scissor-tailed Flycatcher
❏ Fork-tailed Flycatcher

Shrikes
❏ Loggerhead Shrike

Vireos
❏ White-eyed Vireo
❏ Bell's Vireo
❏ Yellow-throated Vireo
❏ Blue-headed Vireo
❏ Warbling Vireo
❏ Philadelphia Vireo
❏ Red-eyed Vireo

Jays & Crows
❏ Blue Jay
❏ American Crow
❏ Fish Crow
❏ Common Raven

Larks
❏ Horned Lark

Swallows
❏ Purple Martin
❏ Tree Swallow
❏ Northern Rough-winged Swallow
❏ Bank Swallow
❏ Cliff Swallow
❏ Cave Swallow
❏ Barn Swallow

Chickadees & Titmice
❏ Carolina Chickadee
❏ Tufted Titmouse

Nuthatches
❏ Red-breasted Nuthatch
❏ White-breasted Nuthatch
❏ Brown-headed Nuthatch

Creepers
❏ Brown Creeper

Wrens
❏ Carolina Wren
❏ Bewick's Wren

❑ House Wren
❑ Winter Wren
❑ Sedge Wren
❑ Marsh Wren

Kinglets
❑ Golden-crowned Kinglet
❑ Ruby-crowned Kinglet

Gnatcatchers
❑ Blue-gray Gnatcatcher

Bluebirds & Thrushes
❑ Eastern Bluebird
❑ Veery
❑ Gray-cheeked Thrush
❑ Bicknell's Thrush
❑ Swainson's Thrush
❑ Hermit Thrush
❑ Wood Thrush
❑ American Robin
❑ Varied Thrush

Mimic Thrushes
❑ Gray Catbird
❑ Northern Mockingbird
❑ Brown Thrasher

Starlings
❑ European Starling

Wagtails & Pipits
❑ White Wagtail
❑ American Pipit
❑ Sprague's Pipit

Waxwings
❑ Cedar Waxwing

Wood-warblers
❑ Bachman's Warbler
❑ Blue-winged Warbler
❑ Golden-winged Warbler
❑ Tennessee Warbler
❑ Orange-crowned Warbler
❑ Nashville Warbler
❑ Northern Parula
❑ Yellow Warbler
❑ Chestnut-sided Warbler
❑ Magnolia Warbler
❑ Cape May Warbler

❑ Black-throated Blue Warbler
❑ Yellow-rumped Warbler
❑ Black-throated Gray Warbler
❑ Black-throated Green Warbler
❑ Blackburnian Warbler
❑ Yellow-throated Warbler
❑ Pine Warbler
❑ Kirtland's Warbler
❑ Prairie Warbler
❑ Palm Warbler
❑ Bay-breasted Warbler
❑ Blackpoll Warbler
❑ Cerulean Warbler
❑ Black-and-white Warbler
❑ American Redstart
❑ Prothonotary Warbler
❑ Worm-eating Warbler
❑ Swainson's Warbler
❑ Ovenbird
❑ Northern Waterthrush
❑ Louisiana Waterthrush
❑ Kentucky Warbler
❑ Connecticut Warbler
❑ Mourning Warbler
❑ Common Yellowthroat
❑ Hooded Warbler
❑ Wilson's Warbler
❑ Canada Warbler
❑ Yellow-breasted Chat

Tanagers
❑ Summer Tanager
❑ Scarlet Tanager
❑ Western Tanager

Sparrows & Allies
❑ Green-tailed Towhee
❑ Spotted Towhee
❑ Eastern Towhee
❑ Bachman's Sparrow
❑ American Tree Sparrow
❑ Chipping Sparrow
❑ Clay-colored Sparrow
❑ Field Sparrow
❑ Vesper Sparrow
❑ Lark Sparrow
❑ Lark Bunting
❑ Savannah Sparrow

❏ Grasshopper Sparrow
❏ Henslow's Sparrow
❏ Le Conte's Sparrow
❏ Nelson's Sharp-tailed Sparrow
❏ Saltmarsh Sharp-tailed Sparrow
❏ Seaside Sparrow
❏ Fox Sparrow
❏ Song Sparrow
❏ Lincoln's Sparrow
❏ Swamp Sparrow
❏ White-throated Sparrow
❏ Harris's Sparrow
❏ White-crowned Sparrow
❏ Dark-eyed Junco
❏ Lapland Longspur
❏ Smith's Longspur
❏ Snow Bunting

Cardinals, Grosbeaks & Buntings
❏ Northern Cardinal
❏ Rose-breasted Grosbeak
❏ Black-headed Grosbeak
❏ Blue Grosbeak
❏ Lazuli Bunting
❏ Indigo Bunting

❏ Painted Bunting
❏ Dickcissel

Blackbirds & Allies
❏ Bobolink
❏ Red-winged Blackbird
❏ Eastern Meadowlark
❏ Western Meadowlark
❏ Yellow-headed Blackbird
❏ Rusty Blackbird
❏ Brewer's Blackbird
❏ Common Grackle
❏ Boat-tailed Grackle
❏ Shiny Cowbird
❏ Brown-headed Cowbird
❏ Orchard Oriole
❏ Bullock's Oriole
❏ Baltimore Oriole

Finches
❏ Purple Finch
❏ House Finch
❏ Red Crossbill
❏ White-winged Crossbill
❏ Common Redpoll
❏ Pine Siskin
❏ American Goldfinch
❏ Evening Grosbeak

Old World Sparrows
❏ House Sparrow

Select References

American Ornithologists' Union. 1998. *Check-list of North American Birds.* 7th ed. (and its supplements). American Ornithologists' Union, Washington, D.C.

Potter, E.F. *et al.* 2006. *Birds of the Carolinas.* Second edition. University of North Carolina Press, Chapel Hill.

Robin, M. 1993. *Finding Birds in South Carolina.* University of South Carolina Press, Columbia, SC.

Sibley, D.A. 2002. *Sibley's Birding Basics.* Alfred A. Knopf, New York.

Index

Boat-tailed Grackle